SHAKESPEARE'S
GLOBE

BUILDING
HISTORY
SERIES

SHAKESPEARE'S
GLOBE

by Amy Allison

Lucent Books, Inc., San Diego, California

Library of Congress Cataloging-in-Publication Data

Allison, Amy, 1956–
 Shakespeare's Globe / by Amy Allison.
  p.   cm. — (Building history series)
 Includes bibliographical references (p.   ) and index.
 Summary: Discusses the history of Shakespeare's Globe
Theatre, including its construction, the plays that were
performed there, its financial aspects, and the reconstruction
in 1995.
  ISBN 1-56006-526-5 (alk. paper)
  1. Globe Theatre (Southwark, London, England) Juvenile
literature.   2. Shakespeare, William, 1564–1616—Stage
history—England—London Juvenile literature.   3. Shakespeare,
William, 1564–1616—Stage history—To 1625 Juvenile literature.
4. Theater—England—London—History—17th Century Juvenile
literature.   5. Theaters—England—London Juvenile literature.
[1. Globe Theatre (Southwark, London, England)   2. Shakespeare, William, 1564–1616—Stage history.   3. Theaters—
History.]   I. Title.   II. Series.
PR2920.A56   2000
792'.09421'6409031—dc21   99-27313
                                                                          CIP

Copyright 2000 by Lucent Books, Inc.
P.O. Box 289011, San Diego, California, 92198-9011

Printed in the U.S.A.

CONTENTS

FOREWORD

Throughout history, as civilizations have evolved and prospered, each has produced unique buildings and architectural styles. Combining the need for both utility and artistic expression, a society's buildings, particularly its large-scale public structures, often reflect the individual character traits that distinguish it from other societies. In a very real sense, then, buildings express a society's values and unique characteristics in tangible form. As scholar Anita Abramovitz comments in her book *People and Spaces*, "Our ways of living and thinking—our habits, needs, fear of enemies, aspirations, materialistic concerns, and religious beliefs—have influenced the kinds of spaces that we build and that later surround and include us."

That specific types and styles of structures constitute an outward expression of the spirit of an individual people or era can be seen in the diverse ways that various societies have built palaces, fortresses, tombs, churches, government buildings, sports arenas, public works, and other such monuments. The ancient Greeks, for instance, were a supremely rational people who originated Western philosophy and science, including the atomic theory and the realization that the earth is a sphere. Their public buildings, epitomized by Athens's magnificent Parthenon temple, were equally rational, emphasizing order, harmony, reason, and above all, restraint.

By contrast, the Romans, who conquered and absorbed the Greek lands, were a highly practical people preoccupied with acquiring and wielding power over others. The Romans greatly admired and readily copied elements of Greek architecture, but modified and adapted them to their own needs. "Roman genius was called into action by the enormous practical needs of a world empire," wrote historian Edith Hamilton. "Rome met them magnificently. Buildings tremendous, indomitable, amphitheaters where eighty thousand could watch a spectacle, baths where three thousand could bathe at the same time."

In medieval Europe, God heavily influenced and motivated the people, and religion permeated all aspects of society, molding people's worldviews and guiding their everyday actions. That spiritual mindset is reflected in the most important medieval structure—the Gothic cathedral—which, in a sense, was a model of heavenly cities. As scholar Anne Fremantle so elegantly phrases it, the cathedrals were "harmonious elevations of stone and glass reaching up to heaven to seek and receive the light [of God]."

Our more secular modern age, in contrast, is driven by the realities of a global economy, advanced technology, and mass communications. Responding to the needs of international trade and the growth of cities housing millions of people, today's builders construct engineering marvels, among them towering skyscrapers of steel and glass, mammoth marine canals, and huge and elaborate rapid transit systems, all of which would have left their ancestors, even the Romans, awestruck.

In examining some of humanity's greatest edifices, Lucent Books' Building History series recognizes this close relationship between a society's historical character and its buildings. Each volume in the series begins with a historical sketch of the people who erected the edifice, exploring their major achievements as well as the beliefs, customs, and societal needs that dictated the variety, functions, and styles of their buildings. A detailed explanation of how the selected structure was conceived, designed, and built, to the extent that this information is known, makes up the majority of the volume.

Each volume in the Lucent Building History series also includes several special features that are useful tools for additional research. A chronology of important dates gives students an overview, at a glance, of the evolution and use of the structure described. Sidebars create a broader context by adding further details on some of the architects, engineers, and construction tools, materials, and methods that made each structure a reality, as well as the social, political, and/or religious leaders and movements that inspired its creation. Useful maps help the reader locate the nations, cities, streets, and individual structures mentioned in the text; and numerous diagrams and pictures illustrate tools and devices that bring to life various stages of construction. Finally, each volume contains two bibliographies, one for student research, the other listing works the author consulted in compiling the book.

Taken as a whole, these volumes, covering diverse ancient and modern structures, constitute not only a valuable research tool, but also a tribute to the human spirit, a fascinating exploration of the dreams, skills, ingenuity, and dogged determination of the great peoples who shaped history.

IMPORTANT DATES IN THE BUILDING OF SHAKESPEARE'S GLOBE

1576
The Theatre, the first privately managed, self-supporting playhouse, opens in the London suburb of Shoreditch.

1603
The Globe's company is appointed by Elizabeth's successor, James I, as his own royal players and renamed the King's Men.

1599
The Globe, completed by May, launches its initial season of plays.

1608
The King's Men take up winter residence at the Blackfriars, an indoor theater, leading to the Globe's eventual eclipse as the troupe's principal playhouse.

| 1575 | 1585 | 1595 | 1605 | 1615 |

1601
The Globe's players present Shakespeare's politically charged *Richard II*, risking implication in a revolt by the earl of Essex.

1598
Under cover of night, on December 28, the Theatre is dismantled and its timbers transported to the Bankside property, south of London, where it will be resurrected as the Globe.

8

Construction of the new Globe theater in London.

1614
By the summer, the Globe is rebuilt on its old foundation, this time with a nonflammable tile roof.

1642
Upon the outbreak of civil war pitting King Charles I against Parliament, London's playhouses are shut down.

| 1615 | 1625 | 1635 | 1645 | 1995 |

1613
The Globe burns to the ground during a performance, when a cannon is fired as the Elizabethan equivalent of a special effect.

1643
The Globe is demolished to make way for public housing.

1996
A new Globe playhouse launches a theatrical career on familiar territory: London's Bankside.

1624
Authorities order the closing of the Globe's successful run of Thomas Middleton's *Game at Chesse,* a play critical of the Crown's policy toward Spain.

9

INTRODUCTION

Beginning in Italy in the fourteenth century, the movement known as the Renaissance developed from an intense interest in the classical cultures of ancient Greece and especially Rome. Old and new ideas circulated freely, sparking a burst of creativity in science and art.

The Renaissance reached England in the sixteenth century, during the reign of Elizabeth I, the last and greatest Tudor monarch. Elizabeth's father, Henry VIII, had paved the way for the spirit of the English Renaissance by striking a blow for the pursuit of personal ambition, defying as he did the hugely powerful Roman Catholic Church. Eager to shed one wife and acquire another, and forbidden to do so by church decree, Henry boldly declared England free of church authority. Church lands were promptly seized by the Crown and made available to enterprising, resourceful Englishmen. These were men willing to toil and scheme to own property and thus achieve the status such ownership gained them.

As a result of all this enterprise, England experienced an economic boom when Henry's successor, Elizabeth, sat on the throne. Elizabeth herself promoted the nation's economic expansion not only by avoiding costly wars but by establishing England's command of the seas—and therefore the control of highly profitable commercial trade routes. The peace and prosperity of her long reign granted her subjects the time and financial means to support the arts: by attending plays, for example. In addition, the queen, by her own example, cultivated the artistic flowering that marked the English Renaissance. Elizabeth frequently summoned musicians, poets, and actors to entertain at court, demonstrating for her subjects the fashionability of the performing arts.

The greatest artistic achievement of the English Renaissance was its literature, especially its drama. In the 1580s, a group of classically educated young playwrights known as the University Wits transformed English theater. Traditional plays employing stock religious themes gave way to dramatic explorations of individuals struggling with life's complexities. Reflecting the fantasies, hopes, and fears of Elizabethans, English Renaissance theater became a significant social force. It attracted not only large audiences from all classes of society, but also opponents, such as religious and political officials, shocked over its influence.

Housing this social force were the public playhouses, chief among them the Globe. Here numerous plays of William Shakespeare, the leading Elizabethan playwright, were first produced. Shakespeare, responsive to the trends of his day, alluded throughout his plays to classical myth and lore. Reflecting this same trend, the design of the Globe recalled the amphitheaters of the ancient world. Adapted by Tudor craftsmen to forms and techniques of English carpentry, these amphitheaters inspired the tiered, open-aired, horseshoe-shaped Globe and other public playhouses of Elizabethan London.

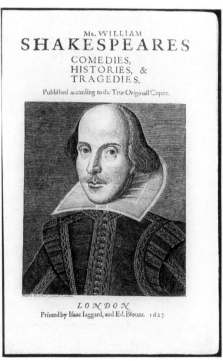

Because playhouse design, playwriting, and production techniques are interrelated, understanding the Globe's design and operation contributes to appreciating a Shakespeare play. Shakespeare clearly presented dramatic devices, as well as dialogue, with the theater's design in mind. Shakespeare's plays show evidence of both the limitations and opportunities the Globe offered to a playwright.

But Shakespeare did more than create plays for the Globe—he also helped finance and manage it. The Globe is significant not only as the theater where some of the best-known plays in the world were first performed, but also as a revolutionary business enterprise. As pointed out by theater historian Peter Thomson,

As the leading Elizabethan playwright, William Shakespeare wrote numerous plays that were performed at the Globe theater.

"For the first time in England, and perhaps anywhere in the world, a theatre was to be built on land leased by the actors, paid for by the actors, and designed by the actors."[1]

As the primary Elizabethan playhouse and instrument of Shakespeare, the Globe represents the spirit of an age eager to explore the world's far-ranging wonders. Within the Globe's

Among the many public playhouses in the Elizabethan period, the Globe featured the first performances of some of the best-known plays the world has ever seen.

walls, the human drama was played out in a multitude of characters and settings. It is no surprise that because of its name and the fact that its stage stood between a roof known as the "heavens" and a cellar housing demons, the Globe has been imagined by some as a model of the world. This idea is echoed in a poem by Thomas Heywood, introducing his 1612 *Apology for Actors:* "If then the world a theatre present, / As by the roundness it appears most fit, / Built with star-galleries of high ascent, / . . . He that denies then theatres should be, / He may as well deny a world to me."[2]

PROLOGUE

In medieval England, an entire village formed the theater for seasonal dramatic festivals known as mystery cycles. Made up of a series of plays recounting biblical stories from Creation to the Resurrection, each mystery cycle took its name for the particular town where it originated—for instance, the Chester Cycle was produced in Chester, a town in northwest England. Production of the cycles absorbed the energies of the town guilds, or craft associations, and each guild performed a play portraying an episode of the cycle appropriate to its craft. For example, the bakers would have presented a depiction of the Last Supper, and the masons and carpenters, the building of the temple in Jerusalem. Stages, each mounted on what were known as pageant wagons, were hauled through the streets of the town in procession. At prearranged points along the procession route, a pageant wagon would halt and guild members would act on its stage the episode for which it had been built.

In the fifteenth century the reign of England's Henry VIII put an end to the mystery cycles because of their association with the Roman Catholic Church, whose authority the king had rejected. With the banishment of this popular form of amateur theater, the performance of plays was increasingly becoming a business conducted by professionals.

An additional reason for the English theater's turning professional was the development of a particular kind of play whose versatility required highly skilled performers. Called an interlude, it was initially performed to entertain guests during the courses of a banquet in the hall of a castle or manor house. But interludes were not only staged in the shelter of a great hall. Traveling players performed such plays throughout the countryside wherever a makeshift stage and booth, or tent, for costume changes could be assembled, such as in a fairground, courtyard, or town square.

LONDON BOUND

Eager for profits, professional players naturally gravitated to where the audiences were, and in sixteenth-century England, as business and commerce flourished, a majority of the audience was to be found in the port city of London. From 1530 to 1605, the city's population more than quadrupled. The difficulty was finding space to perform in such a crowded location.

Fortunately, the London inn yard, an area outlined by the inn's adjoining buildings, was readily adaptable to play performance. Installed at one side of the yard was a platform stage backed by a booth, a curtained-off area for costume changes.

In medieval England, stages mounted on what were called pageant wagons were hauled through the streets of town.

Inn yards were used for performances of plays because audiences could view the play from the courtyard or pay extra to sit in the balconies.

Audience members stood in the courtyard around the stage or, after paying an additional fee, climbed stairs to seats in upper rooms or balconies for a better view. A general admission fee was collected at the narrow archway serving as the entrance to the yard.

The comparative ease of fee collection was a distinct advantage when performing in an inn yard. Money gathering was a constant problem in outdoor performances in towns and villages, where audiences could quickly disperse once the play was over. Common were strategies such as this one employed by the players of the medieval play *Mankind:* Stop the performance at an exciting moment to press the audience for payment before resuming.

A drawback to performing in inn yards was that innkeepers demanded a portion of the earnings. Also, actors shared the inn yard with carters, or workers who on appointed schedules distributed mail and packages arriving in London. Performances were therefore limited to three days a week. To prosper, an acting troupe needed a base of operations, specifically, a building devoted to presenting plays. In Elizabethan times, circumstances and personalities were converging to make that happen.

A COMEBACK FOR CLASSICISM

The cultural movement known today as the Renaissance, meaning "rebirth," began sweeping through Europe in the fifteenth century. Sparked by the rediscovery of ancient texts written in Greek and Latin, the Renaissance brought a renewed interest in Greek and Roman literature and drama, as well as art and architecture. Reaching England during the Elizabethan Age, that is, between the mid–sixteenth through the early seventeenth centuries, the Renaissance there centered on the theater. For inspiration, the Elizabethans looked to the glories of Greek and Roman theater.

In the 1500s, ruins of stone amphitheaters, remnants of Roman occupation centuries earlier, could still be found scattered about the English countryside. Still, it is Elizabethan mathematician and astrologer John Dee who is often credited with bringing principles of Greco-Roman architecture to the attention of his contemporaries. In this endeavor, Dee drew on a classical source, *De Architectura,* written by the Roman architect Marcus Vitruvius Pollio sometime around 27 B.C. A handbook for practicing architects and engineers of the time, *De Architectura* discussed civic architecture, including theater construction.

Vitruvius's main concern in theater construction was acoustics. Striving to maximize the audience's ability to hear the players' words in every part of the theater, he drew on his principles, derived from those of the ancient Greeks. The Greeks of classical times based the semicircular design of their theaters on their understanding of how sound travels: in waves of air radiating from a central point, illustrated by the rippling caused when a pebble is tossed into water. As described by Dee, "the ancient architects, following in the footsteps of nature, perfected the ascending rows of seats in theatres from their investigations of the ascending voice."[3]

Dee's discussion of Vitruvian principles, appearing as a preface to a translation of the writings of the ancient Greek mathemetician Euclid, was written in English as opposed to Latin, the "learned language" of the day. Dee's comments were thus addressed less to scholars than to ambitious professionals in the building trade, providing new applications of the geometry they already knew from practical experience. The enthusiasm that Dee's popularization of classical principles generated among builders at the time is suggested by the remarks of Robert Stickells, a joiner, or carpenter, and mason active during the Elizabethan period: "These things [the proportions of the building of which he has been speaking] consisteth in man himself, for that man is the proportional and Reasonable creature, & therefore whatsoever is done without these Rules or proportion, is but uncertain matter."[4] In other words, buildings ideally reflect, in

The Elizabethans looked to the ruins of Greek and Roman amphitheaters for inspiration when building their own theaters.

ON ARCHITECTURE

Roman architect and engineer Marcus Vitruvius Pollio authored his *De Architectura (On Architecture)* around 27 B.C., during the reign of Emperor Augustus, to whom the work is dedicated. *De Architectura* is the only direct source of information about ancient theater building available to people today. Since its rediscovery and translation some time in the fifteenth century, it has greatly influenced architecture in the Western world. The neoclassical building style, adapted during the Renaissance from classical principles as interpreted through *De Architectura,* dominated Europe for hundreds of years.

Intended as a handbook for practicing architects, *De Architectura* covers a wide range of subjects, from city planning to philosophy and astrology. Vitruvius advises his readers on building materials, mechanical devices, geometry, measurement, and the qualifications of an architect. Book Five details how to build a theater, and in his emphasis on acoustics, the author encourages architects to study music "that the voice of the players . . . might come more clear & pleasant, to the ears of the lookers on." Among his more practical ideas for improving acoustics is the use of a roof or canopy as a reflecting surface over the stage. Such surfaces in theaters help make the actors' words more audible by directing the sound of their voices out to an audience rather than losing it to the surrounding air.

geometric terms, the human body, a concept derived from Vitruvius. The opportunity to apply such principles to Elizabethan theater construction would not be long in coming.

A PATENT AND A PLAYHOUSE

A favorite of Queen Elizabeth I, the earl of Leicester was the sponsor of an acting company bearing his name, Leicester's Men, whose leader was James Burbage. Quite possibly because Leicester was a favorite of the queen, the Leicester's Men on May 7, 1574, became the first company of players awarded royal letters of patent, granting them the right to perform in London and elsewhere "as well for the recreation of [the queen's] loving subjects as for her own solace and enjoyment."[5]

Burbage was emboldened by his company's patent even as he chafed under the harassment of London authorities, who were maneuvering for the right to censor plays. As a result, he pursued his ambition to construct an independently managed, self-supporting playhouse, financed not by public or royal funds but by individual investors. And he would construct it outside the city limits. Not only were plots of land in the areas surrounding London comparatively inexpensive, but they lay beyond the reaches of London's mayor and city council.

Burbage settled for the site of his theater on Shoreditch, located about a mile north of London. Like most of suburban London at that time, Shoreditch was something of a slum. The site of Burbage's great theatrical experiment was, when he first laid eyes on the property, flanked by an open sewer. From these humble surroundings rose the first building in Europe since ancient times purposefully fashioned for the performing of plays. It would be the prototype for the open-air public playhouse that, according to Simon Trussler, "was the single innovation without which the so-called 'golden age' of the Elizabethan drama could scarcely have occurred."[6]

A FORTUNATE COINCIDENCE

A supporter of the sciences as well as the arts, the earl of Leicester was a sponsor not only of James Burbage and his acting company but also of John Dee. Scholars have therefore speculated that Burbage may have been acquainted with Dee and consequently with Vitruvius's ideas in *De Architectura.* Such an acquaintance, the theory goes, may have guided Burbage in the plan for his playhouse.

Dee's guidance would certainly have helped Burbage make sense of *De Architectura.* Versions of the work then available left plenty of room for interpretation. The work in its original form, with its numerous illustrations clarifying points made by Vitruvius, had been long lost. It was difficult enough to grasp the author's intent in surviving copies written in the original Latin—reading Vitruvius in translation created even more opportunity for misunderstanding.

Much guesswork, therefore, went into determining the principles of Greco-Roman design as laid out by Vitruvius, principles that Elizabethans were eager to imitate. Most likely, Burbage's playhouse was a melding of guesswork and familiar, tried-and-true English carpentry techniques.

ENTERPRISE—ELIZABETHAN STYLE

A carpenter by training, Burbage undoubtedly fancied himself suited to the task of crafting a playhouse. In Elizabethan times, masons and carpenters in supervisory roles increasingly functioned as architects, often determining the design as well as construction of buildings. In addition to understanding the principles of building, as an actor Burbage would have understood what a performance space required. Finally, as the manager of a theatrical troupe, he was well aware of what features would gain his venture financial success.

An existing structure that probably influenced Burbage in planning his theater was the baiting house, an arena where, in a horrifying display of cruelty, chained bulls and, more often, bears were viciously set upon by hounds. Also called gaming houses or baiting rings, these wooden amphitheaters defined a circular pit about sixty or more feet in diameter. Their tiered open structure was likely borrowed from antiquity—particularly considering the association of bloody animal "sport" with Roman arenas. Although no record exists of play performances being held in baiting rings during Burbage's lifetime, he would

JOHN DEE

Appearing in 1570, Dee's preface to an English translation of the writings of the ancient Greek mathematician Euclid contributed greatly to advances in science and technology during the Elizabethan Age. Dee understood mathematics' importance to the study and application of science, as suggested by the description of this work on its title page: a "very fruitful Preface made by Master John Dee, specifying the chief Mathematical Sciences, what they are, and whereunto commodious; where also, are disclosed certain new Secrets Mathematical and Mechanical, until these our days greatly missed." Dee's discussion of how geometry could improve technology and encourage invention made a great impact on ambitious members of the Elizabethan middle class who were eager to make a name for themselves in their trades, including the building trades of carpentry and masonry.

Gaming houses, where entertainment consisted of bears being viciously attacked by hounds, probably influenced the design of James Burbage's playhouse, known simply as "The Theatre."

certainly have been familiar with the rings themselves. Between 1546 and 1576, six of these gaming houses stood in the Bankside, on the south bank of the Thames River.

Especially significant for the profit-minded Burbage would have been the baiting rings' large audience capacity. Although smaller in scale than the vast amphitheaters of the ancients, their roughly rounded floor plan accommodated many more spectators than did the rectangular inn yards. Not only was the pit area greater in the baiting house, but higher-priced gallery seating nearly surrounded the action rather than being available only here and there, as in an upper-story room overlooking the inn yard. Even better, the tiered seating arrangement of the baiting rings allowed many audience members to see more than the back of someone's head—and to pay for that privilege.

PARADIGM FOR A PLAYHOUSE

Whatever the inspiration for the playhouse's design, once it was open for business Londoners seemed more than willing to trek farther than a mile from their homes to be entertained in what

Burbage's theater—with its stage, tiered galleries, open yard, and pillars—was the first structure of its kind.

Burbage dubbed "The Theatre." Building a permanent home for an acting troupe was helping to transform theater into a professional institution, so, writes theater historian Simon Trussler, "instead of the theatre going to the people, the people of London were now able to go to The Theatre."[7] Samuel Kiechel, a German visitor and playgoer in 1584, noted that "a great number of people always enters to see such entertainments" in what he termed "peculiar houses."[8] Kiechel's perception of the playhouses in England as "peculiar" suggests that nothing like them existed elsewhere in Europe. In fact, no other building before

Burbage's had ever been called a "theater," a French term that to contemporary ears probably sounded fancy and sophisticated.

The Theatre evidently consisted of a large wooden frame surrounding a raised platform—the stage—and a "backstage" booth. The Theatre's three tiered galleries, covered by an overhang, faced an open yard and a large rectangular platform stage. Supported on trestles or supports, the stage was lifted five-and-a-half to six feet above the ground—slightly above eye level of the average adult spectator.

The booth at the rear of the stage, known as a tiring-house (or "attiring" ["dressing"] house), was set into the building's frame. It served as a storage as well as dressing area. Large props meant to establish locale during a play—a bed, for example, signifying a bedroom—would have been stored there in order to be brought onstage quickly and easily.

As an improvement over the makeshift medieval booth, doors were installed in the facade of the tiring-house for protection against the weather. A flat canopy, supported by pillars, covered the stage to shield it (and the actors) from sun, wind, and rain. To provide for efficient drainage of rainwater, the area surrounding the stage was paved with stone or heavy-duty mortar. Otherwise, in wet weather, it would have been churned into mud by the feet of the "groundlings," those audience members who stood in front and around the sides of the stage.

FAMILY BUSINESS

Designing a theater was one thing, coming up with the money to build it another. Rich in ambition as Burbage may have been, he was not a wealthy man. Even mortgaging his lease on the Shoreditch property would not entirely finance the building of his theater. He still lacked money for materials and workers' wages.

Fortunately, his wife's brother, John Brayne, a prosperous grocer, was willing to pursue any opportunity for profit. Brayne therefore agreed to join in his brother-in-law's enterprise, sharing equally in expenses and earnings. Yet even with Brayne's contribution, the cost of realizing Burbage's ambitions exceeded his available funds. Although not quite finished, the Theatre was forced to open in 1576. Its earnings would be used for completing construction.

Even close family relationships can be strained when money is involved. Burbage's partnership with his brother-in-law eventually deteriorated into a bitter series of legal battles—essentially over dividing up profits from their joint venture—that continued even after their deaths, to be settled eventually in favor of Burbage's heirs. The battle turned into a brawl on at least one occasion when, in 1590, the entire Burbage family—James, his wife, Ellen, and their two sons, Cuthbert and Richard—fended off an attempted takeover of the playhouse by supporters of Brayne's widow.

DEAR LANDLORD

Burbage also provoked the enmity of Gyles Allen, the owner of the property on which the Theatre stood. In 1582, a party suing Allen over ownership of the Shoreditch property conspired to seize the grounds by force, thereby disrupting performances at the Theatre. Burbage, whose life had been endangered on one occasion in defense of the property, hired guards to patrol the grounds. To cover that expense, Burbage withheld a portion of his rent from Allen. Burbage and Allen fought over this for the next fifteen years.

As the twenty-one-year lease on the property drew to a close, Allen schemed to add to the renewal conditions that Burbage recognized were meant to disrupt his theatrical enterprise. These included a rent increase of more than 70 percent and the payment of the amount of rent Burbage had withheld—which Allen continued to insist was due him. Allen also demanded a provision that limited the use of the building Burbage had built on the property as a playhouse to only five years of the period of the renewed lease, and then it was required to be converted to tenements, or housing units.

Burbage was still in negotiations over renewal of the lease when he died early in 1597, two months before the lease was due to expire. Cuthbert Burbage, as James's elder son, then took over negotiations with Allen. These efforts met evasion after evasion on Allen's part, since if he refused renewal outright, his tenant could, according to a provision in the original lease, "at any time or times before the end of the said term of one and twenty years, to have, take down and carry away to his own proper use"[9] any structure he might have erected on the land. The possibility of removing the Theatre was no idle threat. Timbers of Elizabethan buildings were slotted and pegged rather than nailed together in the frame, making it possible to move even large structures piece by piece. James Burbage had indeed threatened to remove his theater if the lease were not renewed.

THE PLANNING STAGE

When in 1598 negotiations with Allen broke off, the two Burbage brothers, following through on their father's threat, devised a plan to preserve the business that had supported them for over twenty years. The Burbages proposed that members of the Theatre's acting company, now regrouped as the Chamberlain's Men and forced to perform at the nearby Curtain, contribute to the expense of removing and rebuilding the playhouse in exchange for a share in the profits of the new theater. Five members agreed: Augustine Phillips, Thomas Pope, John Heminge, Will Kempe, and William Shakespeare.

The owner of the property the partners sought to lease happened to be a neighbor of Heminge and Shakespeare. Sir Nicholas Brend had come into possession of the estate upon his father's death—just a few months before the group went property shopping. Brend asked £14, 10 shillings a year for the land, only 10 shillings more than the rent Allen had been charging.

The property was in Southwark, specifically, a neighborhood known as the Bankside. An entertainment center of sorts, the Bankside offered Londoners—besides baiting houses—archery ranges, taverns, and, since 1587 when the Rose playhouse was built there, plays. The area was convenient for playgoers: a short boat ride or a stroll across London Bridge.

The new site of the Chamberlain's Men's playhouse, like the old one, lay outside the control of London's municipal authorities. And, like Shoreditch, its background was a humble one: a dumping ground, and before that, marshland, only recently drained. The Theatre's successor would stand on Maiden Lane, described at the time in a *Survey of London* as "a long straggling place, with ditches on each side."[10]

A BOLD MOVE

Although not formally drawn up and signed until February 21, 1599, the lease on the Bankside property took effect on Christmas Day, 1598. Apparently with Brend's blessing, the company took possession immediately. The Christmas season was an opportune time to carry out their plan of moving the Theatre to its new location. Allen was bound to be away in his country estate for the holidays.

Three days after the start of the lease, the Burbage brothers, accompanied by their mother, master carpenter Peter Streete, and a dozen laborers, proceeded to the Theatre. According to charges subsequently leveled by Allen, the Burbage party did

> riotously assemble themselves together, and then and there armed themselves with diverse and many unlawful and offensive weapons, as namely swords, daggers, bills [hood-shaped blades mounted on staffs], axes, and such like and so armed did then repair to the said Theatre and . . . attempted to pull down the said Theatre . . . and having so done, did then also in most forcible and riotous manner take and carry away from thence all the wood and timber thereof to the Bankside.[11]

SOUTHWARK

At the turn of the seventeenth century, London playgoers flocked to the Bankside, in the district of Southwark, where the newly built Globe soon outrivaled the neighboring Rose and Swan playhouses. Outside the censure of London authorities, the Bankside also offered Londoners "entertainments" in taverns, brothels, and bull- and bear-baiting rings. The district's unsavory reputation was reinforced by its three prisons: King's Bench, Marshalsea, and the Clink, which has lent its name to prisons all over the English-speaking world.

Toward the end of the twentieth century, London's south bank experienced a revival of sorts, beginning with the building of the Royal National Theatre and continuing with the reconstruction of the Globe itself. The area today is dotted with trendy pubs. The George Inn, founded around the time of Queen Elizabeth's father, Henry VIII, still hosts visitors.

Despite Allen's accusations, the presence of master carpenter Streete to supervise the dismantling suggests something more orderly than a wrecking job. For the Theatre to be resurrected as a new playhouse, Streete and his crew must have gone about their work with some care. The survival of the Chamberlain's Men, along with the plays of one of their members by the name of Will Shakespeare, was at stake.

ALL THE WORLD'S A STAGE

On the night the Theatre was dismantled, master carpenter Peter Streete was already busy planning the playhouse's restructuring as the Globe. Examining the Theatre, Streete confirmed that its structural plan was based on a surveyor's, or three-rod, line. Elizabethan builders were also surveyors, or skilled measurers of land, and used the sixteen-foot, six-inch statute rod—known as a perch—as their prime unit of measurement. Valentine Leigh's 1578 *Science of Surveying* praised the line—marked with knots for every perch and "well seared with hot Wax and Rosen, to avoid stretching thereof in the wet, and shrinking in the drought"[12]—for the speed and ease of its use. Because of its apparent use in the layout of the Theatre, the three-rod line would also be the basis for the design of the Globe.

Generally, Elizabethan builders drew up more or less detailed blueprints known as platts. Platts were drawn to scale: A proportion was set up between the dimensions of the drawing and those of the objects they represented to show relative sizes of objects and spaces. For instance, Streete's contract for building the Fortune, a rival to the Globe, mentions an accompanying platt (which unfortunately has not survived).

Streete's building plans for the Globe apparently consisted of the notes he made at the Theatre site, augmented by his knowledge of mathematics and geometry. Using his surveyor's line, Streete would have measured the Theatre's frame with the intention of reassembling it at the Bankside. The foundations he and his crew built to underlie the new playhouse would need to be the right size to accept the recycled timber frame from the old building. Then as the frame went up, Streete would have checked and rechecked its dimensions to ensure their accuracy.

WHEN IS A CIRCLE NOT A CIRCLE?

The basic frame of the Globe may appear round in the long-distance sketches of it that survive, but was it in fact shaped that way? A round, or rounded, building was certainly best for enabling as many playgoers as possible to see and hear a performance well.

However, constructing a circular building out of wood would have required substantially more material and labor and therefore increased the cost. Even if cost had not been a concern, a timber frame could not be made truly round without weakening it. Curved timbers are incapable of carrying as much weight as straight ones. "Wood does not lend itself readily to curved lines," explains Shakespearean scholar John Cranford Adams.

GEOMETRY

Evidently, geometry was applied in planning the Globe. Theater scholar John Orrell believes that Peter Streete used a method relying on practical geometry, known as *ad quadratum*, in laying out and constructing the playhouse. Orrell describes how this method, familiar to medieval carpenters, works.

> Medieval builders worked most of all from the geometry of circles, squares and triangles. Their commonest trick was that of *ad quadratum* design: one part of a building would be the length of a square whose diagonal provided the dimension of another, related part. As, for example, the length and width of a room. A variation . . . was to make a circle equal to the whole diameter of the building. Inside it the carpenter drew a square, its corners touching the circle; inside that square he drew a smaller circle, whose perimeter just touched the sides of the square. Now the smaller circle was proportioned *ad quadratum* to the larger one (in fact its diameter was equal to the larger one, divided by 2). It wasn't always necessary to work all this out in a drawing, because certain numerical series were well-known as approximations of the proportions . . . for example, . . . the one used at the roof level of the Globe—70:99. The diameter of the Globe was 99 feet . . . while its top part . . . was 70 feet. A perfectly traditional *ad quadratum* design.

"The heavy beams required in the main frame of so large a structure [as the Globe]—unlike the relatively slender ribs of a boat—cannot be bent to a curve, however flat."[13]

The alternative was to construct a many-sided, or polygonal, building, which from a distance would have appeared rounded. Archaeological evidence suggests the playhouse had twenty sides, so, in preparation for placing the framework of the Globe, a twenty-sided polygon would have been traced on the ground within a circle marked with ropes and pegs. Once the placement of the Globe's frame was determined, construction could begin.

In preparation for placing the framework of the Globe, a twenty-sided polygon was traced on the ground, as seen in this illustration, to give the theater the appearance of being round.

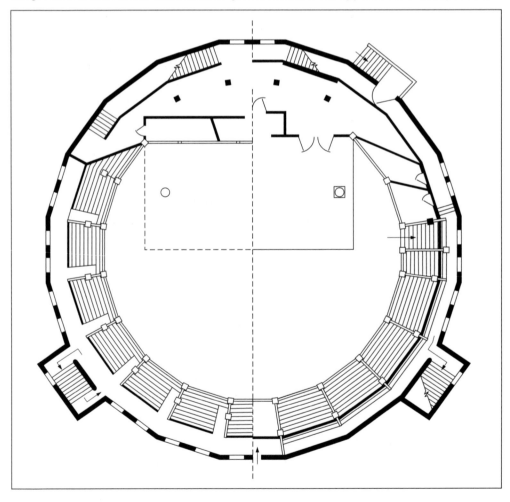

A FIRM FOUNDATION AND FRAME

The weight of the frame for a building as large as an Elizabethan playhouse demanded a sturdy foundation. Bricks, or clay blocks fired to the required hardness, promised solidness and durability. And they resisted dampness. This was crucial because the Globe was to be built on marshland that had only recently been drained. The land's history as a marsh required an extra step before the foundation could be laid. To brace the foundation on the Bankside's soft soil, Streete's crew first sank piles, or large timber columns, on the site. These would be driven into the soil vertically until they reached solid ground or rock and could not be pushed down farther. Upon them the red-brick base would firmly rest.

Once the Globe's foundation was in place, carpenters under Streete's direction could begin erecting the frame. Heavy oak timbers called ground sills were laid lengthwise on the foundation walls, and upright posts were slotted, or inserted, into them to begin forming the frame. The frame was a post-and-lintel construction, which is made of vertical wood posts supporting horizontal lintels or beams. Beams known as binding joists served as "ribs" joining the frame's outer wall to its inner wall. Consisting of two concentric polygonal walls, the frame therefore had depth as well as height and width. This gave it stability without increasing its weight or bulk.

The walls of the Globe theater rose between thirty and thirty-five feet above the ground. As a result, its height measured about a third of its width. Theater scholar Richard Hosley estimates that the bottom of its three galleries, or stories, measured six feet high, the middle gallery a bit less, and the topmost gallery less than that. Adequate height was necessary not only to allow sufficient headroom for playgoers, but also to provide as many of them as possible with an unobstructed view of the stage.

In most timber buildings of the Tudor period, each story projected slightly beyond the story below it. This allowed rain to drip free of the frame, thus keeping water from seeping into the frame's wooden joints and rotting them.

"A DELIGHTFUL IRREGULARITY"

Because of the irregular sizes of the timber used in Elizabethan construction, pieces composing the frames of buildings were not

"DIVINE PROPORTIONS"

Barry Day, in his book *This Wooden "O": Shakespeare's Globe Reborn,* writes of the mystical quality some have attached to the shape and proportions of the playhouse.

Elizabethan scholars, anxiously straddling the divide between medieval thought and the new teachings of Renaissance thinking—which Frances Yates termed the "mystico-magico scientific movement"—sought meaning in everything from grains of earth thrown on the ground to dots on a page. They believed with Hamlet that there was "a special providence in the fall of a sparrow." Science and mysticism were by no means considered incompatible as subjects for study. . . . To people with this mixed mind set, such as the Elizabethan builders, for instance, the proportions of the Globe . . . might well have seemed enchanted, since they appear to correspond to music harmonies.

"Divine proportions," many scholars believed, ran through man and the universe, uniting such apparently diverse subjects as music and mathematics.

"Geometry was at the heart of this building," says [Mark] Rylance [actor and artistic director of the rebuilt Globe]. "The round shape was considered the heart of a human being—the marriage of what you can imagine and what you can do."

interchangeable. Being hand-cut and varying in width, thickness, and straightness, no two timbers were alike, and neither were their joinings. "There was a delightful irregularity and home-spun quality in Tudor design and construction," writes historian Irwin Smith, explaining that the "irregularities inherent in the materials compelled irregularity and improvisation in their use."[14]

Tudor carpenters improvised a system of markers to guide them in assembling—or reassembling—the wooden frames of buildings. Generally, these markers were in two parts: a Roman numeral and a symbol—for example, a crow's foot—grafted onto the numeral. Roman numerals were used because it was easier to carve their straight lines into wood than it would be to carve the curvier lines of Arabic numbers. The symbol identified the wall or part of a wall to which the numeral applied. The system was far from standardized. A single stroke might, to save time, do double duty as part of two numerals: For example, XV might appear as ᛈ or XX as ⚡. Still, the system allowed frameworks to be reassembled without time-consuming trial and error.

Reuse of timber was possible because of the remarkable durability of English oak, the material used almost exclusively in Elizabethan construction. "In times past men were contended to dwell in houses builded of sallow, willow, plum-tree, hard-beame, and elm, so that the use of oak was in a manner dedicated wholly unto churches, religious houses, princes' palaces, noblemen's lodgings, and navigation; but now all these are rejected, and nothing but oak any whit regarded,"[15] observed William Harrison in his 1577 *Description of England*. Recycling oak timbers was also becoming a necessity. England's oak forests were declining because of the demand for timber created by an increasingly prosperous nation.

GADGETS AND GIZMOS

The larger timbers of the Theatre's frame, and possibly the planks used in the flooring of the galleries and the stage, were salvaged. Smaller pieces, however, may not have survived the demolition, so some fresh timbers would have been needed for the Globe. Those timbers would have required shaping to be fit for use by the building crew. According to Smith, the wood surfaces of Elizabethan buildings "showed the honest marks of the tools that shaped them."[16] The adze's thin, arched blade set perpendicular to the handle smoothed and shaped the wood felled by the carpenter's ax. The carpenter also used the ax to square the timbers where they lay to make them easier to transport. The saw, although used since medieval times, was apparently scorned by Elizabethan carpenters, who judged it, according to Alex Beazeley of the Royal Institute of British Architects, "a contemptible innovation fit only for those unskillful in the handling of the nobler instrument,"[17] that is, the ax.

To connect such timbers firmly enough to bear the strains upon them, a bewildering variety of joinings were employed: scarfs, notches, dovetails, and joggles among them. All joinings, though, served to lock one piece to another. A common type of joining was mortise and tenon, or interlocking wood fingers. The Globe's posts, for example, were likely mortised into the ground sills.

Once timbers were fitted together, holes were bored through them with large drills called augers. Round wooden pegs, or dowels, were then driven through the holes, though not all the way. As the fittings loosened, because of the drying of the green, or unseasoned, oak, the pegs were hammered farther into the holes to draw the joints together. Nails were avoided not only because they were scarce and expensive, but also because, no matter how heavy, nails would not have ensured an unbending frame, given the frame's bulky timbers made from unseasoned wood.

A FULL (USAGE) HOUSE

A greater challenge than materials and basic building techniques was fitting together the larger components of the building. Characteristic of Elizabethan construction, each part of the Globe was built independently, and then all the pieces were attached. The playhouse's three-story tiring-house, unlike the frame, was rectangular. A separate, self-standing unit, the tiring-house was set into the frame and evidently projected one or two feet from its inner face.

One feature of Elizabethan buildings was a symmetrically balanced design. Symmetry—in which images on either side of a center line mirror each other in size, shape, and position—represented a sense of order and dignity to the Elizabethan mind. Flanking the first-story facade of the Globe's tiring-house were large, round-topped solid-oak doors, one on the right and one on the left. Each, when open on its hinges, allowed actors—on foot or possibly even riding a chariot—ample space to pass from the tiring-house interior to the stage. Stage directions in plays presented at the Globe often specified that characters enter "severally," that is, from opposite sides of the stage. This type of entrance is more symmetrical than logical, since the simplest direction would be for actors to enter from the same side.

Because the Globe stage lacked sets to signal a change of scene, the existence of two doors helped mark the beginning of a new scene. The characters of the previous scene could leave through one door and enter through the other to indicate a change in their location. Evidence is sketchy, but centered between the two doors was likely a wider, curtained opening. From this central passageway, processions of players as well as the company's bulkier stage properties would have been transferred to and from the stage. These properties may have in-

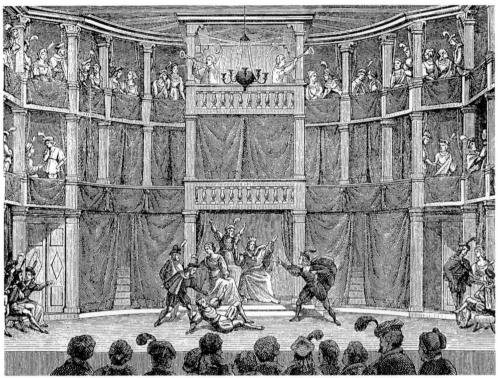

The beginning of a new scene was marked by actors exiting and entering from two side doors on either side of the stage, while a curtained opening in the center was used to bring props onstage.

cluded items such as a canopied bed harboring a "sleeping" actor. Such a third opening would have left the two side doors free for regular entrances and exits by the players.

Openings also appeared in an upper story of the tiring-house that was separated by pillars to form a kind of gallery. This gallery appears to have been occupied, at various times, by spectators, by musicians, or by actors performing "above" the stage. For example, during the balcony scene in *Romeo and Juliet,* the actor playing Juliet (all roles were played by men) positioned himself at a gallery opening, representing a balcony window, to address his lines to his "costar" playing Romeo, standing below on the platform stage.

ON—AND UNDER—THE BOARDS
Also linked with the frame but separate from it was the theater's platform, or stage. The stage's construction would have needed

to be strong and stiff enough to withstand the shrinkage or warping that would have thrown the stage floor out of its true level. It was therefore constructed of a tough, wear-resistant wood, possibly pine, and thoroughly seasoned, or dried, for use.

At forty-three feet across and almost thirty feet deep, the stage had to be strong enough to withstand warping and was elevated to provide a trap-door.

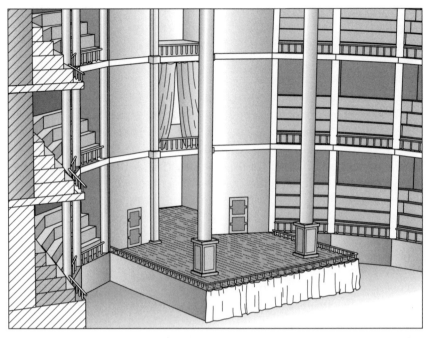

A low railing was put around the edge of the stage to allow actors to judge their distance from the edge and also to keep patrons who sat on the stage from tumbling off.

At forty-three or forty-four feet across and not quite thirty feet front to back, the Globe's stage provided actors with plenty of space to perform—even with audience members now and then taking up room by being seated on it.

A low railing around the edge of the stage evidently helped actors to visually judge their distance from the edge. As a guard rail, it also served to keep those patrons who occasionally sat on the Globe's stage from tumbling into the yard. Built of sturdy oak, the railing was supported by posts, each about eighteen inches high and spaced well apart to avoid seriously blocking the view of audience members standing in the yard. The character of Lucifer in a 1604 Globe play, Thomas Middleton's *Black Book*, refers to this stage feature when, emerging from below the platform, he climbs up onto it and declares,

> And now that I have vaulted up so high
> Above the stage rails of this earthen globe
> I must turn actor and join companies
> To share my comic sleek-eyed villainies.[18]

Supported by trestles, or a series of small, braced timber frameworks, the stage was raised five-and-a-half to six feet above the yard. The average Elizabethan adult stood between five and five-and-a-half feet tall, so the edge of the stage was a bit higher than the tops of the heads of the groundlings—giving those standing closest to the stage a view of the actors' ankles.

The stage's elevation provided enough room for its trapdoor effect, which called for a kind of cellar below. The area under the trapdoor, also known as "hell" because from it ghosts or devils emerged, extended back under the tiring-house and provided passage to and from the dressing room for the actors impersonating these horrors. Around the trap, as few trestles as possible were used to provide easy passage back to the tiring-house. Concealing the workings of "hell," the area below the stage was apparently hung all around with cloth. Evidently, the color of the cloth conveyed the nature of the play being performed that day: red, white, or green for a comedy, black for a tragedy. The anonymous play *A Warning on Fair Women* from about 1590 pronounces, "The stage is hung with black; and I perceive / The auditors prepar'd for tragedie."[19] This cloth covering allowed a reasonable amount of light underneath the stage.

SUPER- AND SUPRASTRUCTURES

If the Globe's stage harbored a "hell," it also boasted a "heavens." This was the name given the stage cover, a kind of wood awning that ran the full length of the tiring-house at the level of its third, or top, story. Sheltering actors underneath it from the discomforts of the weather, the "heavens" was complete with gutters to carry off rainwater. The shade provided to the players by the "shadow"—as the stage cover was also called—was aided by the stage's position with its back to the sun. A player would therefore not be distracted by the need to avoid the sun's glare.

Resting atop the stage cover was a kind of "hut." This attic-like structure was designed primarily to store and operate the winding gear needed to create the theater's flying illusion. It also housed equipment for producing sound effects. The hut, along with the stage cover, made up the Globe's superstructure.

Because the stage cover extended from the base of the hut and sheltered a good portion of the Globe's platform, there was no need to enlarge the hut to provide this covering. Such an enlargement would have significantly added to the superstructure's weight. Streete was therefore able to place supporting posts—at least as the Globe was originally built—well forward and also well apart on the stage. This placement lessened their interference with the audience's view of the action. Rising high above the stage, each post was cut from a single tree trunk. The posts were apparently turned columns (that is, having a vaselike shape).

On the side of the theater opposite the stage—and attached to the frame's outer face, approximately ninety degrees apart—stood two narrow towers that enclosed the theater's staircases. This arrangement, like that of the doorways flanking the tiring-house, presented a visual symmetry that would have appealed to Elizabethans. Because the towers' internal dimensions would not have provided enough space for straight flights of stairs to and from the galleries, the Globe probably had spiral, or "winding," staircases. Located at the foot of each stair tower, the two main entrances to the playhouse were evidently linked by a ground-level passage, running through the frame, to the yard and the first gallery. To best manage the crowd flow, the playhouse's entrances, entryways to the stairs, first gallery, and yard therefore formed a single related unit.

FILLING IN

Once the Globe's frame and interlocking units were firmly in place, workers were ready to begin filling in the spaces in the outer wall between the wood timbers. Half-timber construction, which dominated the Tudor period, consisted of a firm skeleton of oak lumber, framing and supporting whitewashed panels. To fashion these panels, oaken twigs and strips, or laths, were set vertically about fifteen inches apart, their ends wedged into grooves cut into beams in the frame. Hazel wands were then woven through the oak laths to form the latticelike groundwork, or core—known as the wattle—for the daub, or plaster covering.

Two daubers, each working on one side of a playhouse wall, would have applied a coat of plaster over the wattle. Plaster, a pasty substance that dries to a hard finish, has long been used for coating walls and ceilings. The plaster used in the Globe

"MASTER OF BUILDINGS"

In sixteenth-century England, the master mason or carpenter who supervised a building project often functioned as an architect does today. Still, the builder's role in designing a structure depended on how much an employer wanted to interfere. It is difficult to say exactly who designed any building from the Elizabethan period. The plan may have originated with one individual and its architectural rendering and handling with another, and either person may have made modifications once construction was under way. For the practical-minded—and cost-conscious—Elizabethans, what was needed of the newly emerging profession of architect was the ability to visualize a building in such a way that it could easily be altered. Shakespeare alluded to this improvisatory skill around 1598 in *Henry IV, Part II:*

> When we mean to build,
> We first survey the plot, then draw the model;
> And when we see the figure of the house,
> Then must we rate the cost of the erection;
> Which if we find outweighs ability,
> What do we then but draw anew the model . . . ?

consisted of a putty of powdered limestone (or lime), coarse sand, and water; chopped cow hair was also mixed in to help bind the putty to the interwoven laths and wands.

While the first, or base, coat of plaster was still wet, another would have been applied, producing a textured, rather than perfectly smooth, finish. Common since ancient times, plasters made from lime and water add whiteness to a coating and also provide good insulation.

TOPPING IT OFF

The roof sheltering the Globe's hut and galleries was thatched. Rye straw was preferred as a thatching material, because of its length and strength. This would be "stapled" to the rafters—the parallel beams supporting the roof—with bent hazel wands, mostly hidden by the overlaying thatch. In places where the thatch was in danger of being torn away by wind—at the roof's ridge; its eaves, or lower borders; and projecting edges—wands were fastened over it, usually in some decorative pattern such as diamonds. The thatch was laid at least a foot thick.

Because thatch absorbs water, using it as roofing solved the problem of rain dripping from the gallery covering into the playhouse yard—at least during a light shower. During heavy downpours, no plays would have been performed.

Typical of the period, the Globe's roof would have been gabled, that is, having a central ridge and sloping sides. The gable type of roof was strong, its span being short and its design rigid. Its triangular shape was also more of a space saver than a wide, flat, rectangular roof would have been. From the outside, then, the Globe would have looked functional and not at all flashy. The inside would have been another story.

FINISHING TOUCHES

The Elizabethan style of interior decor was shamelessly showy. Carvings and reliefs, or projecting details or figures, as well as embroidered wall hangings very likely decorated the Globe's interior. Eyewitnesses marveled at the "beauty of the houses and the Stages" and alluded to their "gorgeous"[20] decoration.

No doubt the tiring-house facade, the superstructure, and even the stage were painted to cover the exposed woodwork. The color might have been scarlet, yellow, bright orange, any gaudy shade. "The Elizabethans were madmen for painting anything they could get a brush to,"[21] according to architect Jon Greenfield. Painting the Globe's wood surfaces would have made them look like marble and was probably done to suggest a building from classical times. Theater historian John Orrell says that much of the theater would have seemed to be "of expensive colored stone," as "the essence of the place was one of illusion."[22]

Fortunately for the Globe's owners, and their budget, one partner, Richard Burbage, was an accomplished painter. Certainly his most elaborate painting project would have been the underside of the stage cover representing the "heavens," which displayed gold stars, crescent moons, and possibly the signs of the zodiac.

MODESTY ASIDE

The Globe may have been sumptuously decorated, but it failed to offer its audience such creature comforts as toilets. A play, followed by a jig, or lively dance, lasted about three hours, not including the time it took the patrons to settle in and file out. This required playgoers to exercise some control over the calls of nature.

For all their enthusiasm for Renaissance style as they understood it, Elizabethans were still in the Dark Ages when it came to plumbing. Sanitation was especially a problem in towns such as London, where, despite laws against the practice, slop buckets were often simply dumped outside the door. Although the water closet, or toilet, had been invented in 1596, this Elizabethan innovation would have to wait a couple hundred years—when the industrial revolution made piping and sewage practical on a large scale—before coming into use in such public places as theaters.

The Globe, meanwhile, may have supplied buckets for gentlemen to relieve themselves in the open, Elizabethans being more casual about bodily functions than people are today. For the privacy of a "privy," playgoers would have had to make their way to the nearby bank of the Thames, where, according to an engraving at the time, a row of outhouses stood.

A STAR IS BORN

For all the Globe's finery—its lack of comforts and conveniences aside—building the playhouse took only about six months. By May 16, 1599, it was surely completed, as a legal document bearing that date characterizes the Globe as a new building.

Not only did the salvaging of the Theatre's oak framework save the Chamberlain's Men time in the construction of the Globe, but it saved money as well. The total construction cost of the Globe is estimated to have been between £400 and £600. James Burbage and John Brayne earlier had spent £700 to build the Theatre, so the savings for Burbage's sons and the company were substantial.

Yet the Theatre contributed more than building materials to the new playhouse. From it, the Globe inherited a workable design for presenting plays that would in time entertain audiences the world over.

THE PLAY'S THE THING

The silken flag hoisted above an Elizabethan playhouse signaled that a play would be presented that day. Located outside
London, the Globe, along with the other public theaters on the
Bankside south of the Thames, heralded its performances to city
dwellers across the river with these flying banners. As one Lon-
doner wrote in 1612, "Each play-house advanceth his flag in the
air, whither quickly at the waving thereof are summoned whole
troops of men, women and children."[23]

Before the arrival of the audience, the stage would have
been swept clean of dirt and debris. To further ensure that the
stage would be clean and dry during a performance, it was

*A banner flying atop the Globe and other theaters signified to men, women, and children
across the river that a play would be presented that day.*

freshly strewn with rushes, or hollow marsh plants. This covering protected the costly costumes worn by actors who might be called on to sit, lie, fall, or wrestle on the ground in the course of a play. The rushes occasionally represented grassy areas in performances as, for example, in Shakespeare's *A Midsummer Night's Dream,* when a character declares: "This green plot shall be our stage, this hawthorn brake our tyring house."[24] Eventually, plaited-rush matting replaced the rushes.

Though the Globe's audience capacity was perhaps a twentieth that of the great outdoor Greek theaters of ancient times, it was still large. One theater historian, John Orrell, calculates that

TOURIST ATTRACTION

Bustling and prosperous with trade, the port city of London in Elizabethan times attracted foreign visitors. Seeking out novelty, these visitors would have toured the Bankside and its amusements, including the playhouses dotting its shore. In 1599, Thomas Platter, a Swiss scholar, traveled to England, where his itinerary included a performance at the Globe of Shakespeare's *Julius Caesar.* An excerpt of Platter's account of his travels, found in Andrew Gurr's book *Playgoing in Shakespeare's London,* suggests the color and pageantry of an afternoon's entertainment at the Globe.

> On September 21st after lunch, about two o'clock, I and my party crossed the water, and there in the house with the thatched roof witnessed an excellent performance of the tragedy of the first Emperor Julius Caesar with a cast of some fifteen people; when the play was over, they danced very marvellously and gracefully together. . . .

> The actors are most expensively and elaborately costumed; for it is the English usage for eminent lords or knights at their decease to bequeath and leave almost the best of their clothes to the serving men, which it is unseemly for the latter to wear, so that they offer them for sale for a small sum to the actors.

the Globe could have housed about 600 patrons in the yard, nearly 1,000 each in the first and second galleries, and 750 in the top gallery—its usable capacity reduced because of poorer sight lines—for a total of 3,350 paying playgoers. The Spanish ambassador to England wrote about the performance of a brutally anti-Spanish play at the Globe, "there were more than 3,000 persons there on the day that the audience was smallest." He later confirmed that number: "It cannot be pleaded that those who repeat and hear these insults are merely four rogues because during these last four days more than 12,000 persons have all heard the play of *A Game at Chesse,* for so they call it, including all the nobility still in London."[25]

GATHERERS AT THE GATES

The crowd at *A Game at Chesse* was of course exceptional. In a typical week, about 10 percent of London's population of 150,000 attended a play. Playgoers entered the Globe through a door at the foot of one of two stair towers. The narrow doorways ensured that attendees entered single file to keep them from avoiding the penny admission fee, which was paid to a gatherer stationed at either door. The charge doubled to twopence at the opening performance of a new play.

After passing through the door, a playgoer might follow directly along a narrow vestibule, or passageway, running through the Globe's frame to enter the yard. Another option, for those able to pay more for a gallery seat, was to pass through one or two inside doors to the tower stairs. These doors were located at right angles to the main entranceways, so that playgoers—and especially latecomers—could find their way to them quickly and easily. At either doorway, an additional penny would be paid to a second gatherer, allowing the playgoer a place in any of the three galleries. He or she then went up the stairs to the landing at the top of the first flight and entered the first gallery or, if no seating remained there, continued on up to the second gallery.

Seating in the first gallery was best because audience members were at eye level with the actors. If the two lower galleries were filled, the "twopenny" spectator's only option was to climb to the top gallery—evidently a sort of overflow area. Although visibility in the top gallery was limited, for class-conscious patrons it was still preferable to mingling with the poorer classes crowding the yard.

"STINKING FUMES"

Along with consuming snacks and beer, playgoers in the sixteenth and seventeenth centuries often smoked during a performance. The playwright Thomas Dekker, as quoted in Andrew Gurr's book *Playgoing in Shakespeare's London,* describes playhouses populated "with Stinkards who were so glued together in crowds with the Steams of strong breath, that when they came forth, their faces looked as if they had been parboiled."

Tobacco, which had recently been introduced to England from the West Indies by the adventurer Sir Walter Raleigh, quickly became popular with both men and women. It was touted as a cure for all sorts of disorders and apparently served as a kind of narcotic. A cheaper, local version was even developed to meet the demand. In *Playgoing in Shakespeare's London,* an Elizabethan by the name of Henry Buttes is quoted as observing,

It chance'd me gazing at the Theater,
To spy a Lock-Tobacco-Chevalier
Clouding the loathing air with foggy fume
Of Dock-Tobacco, friend foe to rheum.

Corridors, or walkways, ran behind the bleacher-style seats of the galleries, and audience members entered from the rear, stepping down to the best positions toward the front. Since there was no reserved or ticketed seating, to guarantee themselves a good spot, theatergoers came early—or, if they were wealthy enough, sent servants to hold seats for them. Not surprisingly, people would arrive an hour or more before the start of a play to secure a seat, then enjoy a drink of ale or snack on nuts and fruits, which were sold before as well as during a performance.

BEING SEEN AS WELL AS SEEING

If a theatergoer could afford a seat closer to the stage, as well as being more comfortable than on the benches in the galleries, he or she could pass around the corridor behind the first gallery to a "gentlemen's room" bordering the tiring-house. Numbering four in all—two on each side of the tiring-house facade—the gentlemen's rooms were comparable to private boxes in theaters today. These rooms were referred to in 1599 by a Swiss visitor,

Thomas Platter, who explained that if a patron "desires to sit on cushions in the pleasantest place, where he not only sees everything well but can also be seen, then he pays at a further door another English penny."[26]

The nobility often indulged their urge to display themselves and their finery by paying the full fee, of up to twelvepence, and entering by the stage door at the back of the tiring-house, normally used by cast members and other theater personnel. Not only would contact with commoners in the vestibule and gallery be avoided, but the aristocratic playgoer could emerge onto the stage itself to show off in front of the gathering crowd before taking a seat.

This seat might be taken in a lord's room—evidently, in the gallery of the tiring-house, overlooking the stage. Besides providing expensive seats for wealthy playgoers, the lord's room also served as a site for the action of the play. Though the area allowed for only limited movement of actors, it must still have been relatively spacious; a reference from about 1609 describes a card game taking place in the lord's room that involved three or more players.

Alternatively, the privileged playgoer might choose to be seated on a stool on the stage itself. From there, closeness to the action and good sight lines were guaranteed. Perhaps some ten feet on each side of the stage were set aside for these fashionable folk. Although they would interfere with viewing, particularly from the lowermost gallery and yard, the theater's great width prevented them from seriously blocking the entire audience's view.

SITTING VERSUS STANDING

The audience at the Globe was a mixed lot, representing the various classes of society, but where they sat—or stood—was clearly divided along class lines. At the opposite end of the spectrum from privileged patrons sitting above or directly on the stage, laborers, artisans, apprentices, and soldiers were relegated to the open yard. Known as the groundlings, those standing in the yard lacked shelter from either sun or rain. On their feet through an entire performance—which could last three hours without a break—they risked muscle fatigue. To ease the discomfort, the groundlings moved about during the performance, as long as the crowd was not too tightly packed. Hearing and sight lines for those in the yard were far from ideal. From where they stood, the groundlings had to angle their heads somewhat painfully to view the action onstage, while actors' voices passed over their heads.

Apparently, the groundlings were not the only ones in the Globe audience who stood. Most likely, those who arrived too late to find a seat after paying their two pennies were forced to watch the play from a gallery corridor. Unlike playgoers in the yard, however, thanks to the gallery overhangs, these patrons had the benefit of a bit of shelter from the weather. Another advantage over standing in the yard was better sight lines, since audience members in front were seated.

In any case, sitting was preferable to standing: It was less taxing on the body and therefore on the ability to concentrate on the play. Even so, gallery seating must have been cramped, considering that a seated adult takes up at least twice as much space as a standing one. Someone seated in a gallery could expect an area only two feet by two feet to call his or her own. Granted, people in Elizabethan times did tend to be shorter than people are today, but this limited space would have allowed little legroom for a man and scarcely enough room for a woman's ample skirts.

Crowded and cramped, gallery seating—on hard wooden benches without backs—was far from luxurious for those middle-class merchants and lawyers who could afford it. And although the galleries' tiered seating allowed playgoers to see over the heads of people in front of them, sight lines progressively worsened in the middle and topmost levels. Sight lines were unsatisfactory for everyone except those in the first rows of the galleries. Spectators toward the back may have had to bend sideways to see everything onstage.

AN "OPEN" STAGE

In a circular theater the natural direction for the audience to look is toward the center front of the stage. Actors therefore gravitated toward this part of the platform to be better seen as well as heard. In 1615, an observer wrote, "Sit in a full theater, and you will think you see so many lines drawn from the circumference of so many ears, whiles the Actor is the Center."[27]

Because the standing and seating areas of the playhouse curved around the stage, audience members saw the action from different angles. On the Globe's type of thrust, or "open," stage, surrounded on three sides by an audience, actors remained conscious of being in its midst. This sense of intimacy allowed playwrights to use such dramatic devices as asides, direct addresses to the audience, and soliloquies, solo speeches that voice a character's thoughts.

The "open" stage of the Globe offered a sense of intimacy between the actors and the audience, to the point that the audience would cheer, hiss, or shout comments during a performance.

The greater intimacy between the actor and playgoer at the Globe meant that actors had to be on their toes. Audience members reportedly whistled, cheered, booed and hissed, and even shouted out comments during a performance. In such a theater, remarks journalist Richard Covington, "actors need the honed reflexes of a standup comedian; the ability to catch audience banter from out of left field and instantly incorporate it into the action."[28] In 1616, the list of an actor's various accomplishments included "vigilancy," as well as "pregnancy of wit" and "elocution."[29]

Making further demands on the actor's stamina, not to mention his vocal chords, was the requirement to project his voice outdoors. Making oneself heard poses a problem for actors in outdoor theaters, since sound disperses easily in the open air. In addition, at the Globe, the only reflecting surfaces to control the force and direction of the actors' voices were all at one end of the theater: the stage cover and whatever parts of the tiring-house wall were not curtained. These were hard, wood surfaces, which deflected, or bounced, sound out into the playhouse. Cur-

"SCENT"SATIONS

Crowds at Elizabethan playhouses could expect a heavy dose of perfume. Because it was commonly believed that foul odors bred disease, people continually surrounded themselves with perfume as a preventive measure. Rose water was sprinkled onto hands, while heavier kinds of perfume, in powders and pastes, were beaten into hair dressings and rubbed into leather. Perfumed corsets were popular items.

Also contributing to the increase of perfume use during Elizabethan times was the rise in trade. The expansion of trade routes to Asia made quantities of aromatic substances, including civet and musk, available to the English public. The example of Queen Elizabeth, who doused herself with perfume from her wigs to her shoes, greatly increased the fashionability of wearing scents.

Perfume was not only worn but also carried by wealthier audience members in small, often jewel-studded, containers pierced with tiny holes to allow the fragrance to escape. These containers would be held to the nose when unpleasant smells, possibly from an unwashed body close by, threatened to overwhelm the playgoer.

tains, however, being of a soft material, absorbed and dampened sound, as did the bodies of audience members, especially when the playhouse was crowded. The actors, therefore, needed to work hard to be heard over the audience, which could be boisterous, and the vendors hawking food and drink during a performance.

"ON YOUR IMAGINARY FORCES WORK"

Just before the beginning of a play, for a few moments at least, quiet would have reigned at the Globe. A series of trumpet blasts quieted the audience at about two o'clock in the afternoon—a two o'clock start time allowed the Globe's patrons to return home before dark.

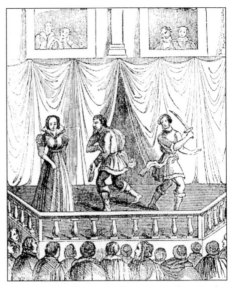

Projecting their voices in order to be heard was a demand on actors who performed in outdoor theaters.

Audience members would have heard the trumpet sound three times: The first announced the readiness of the players, and the second provided an additional warning before the third and final blast signaled the start of the play. The trumpeter apparently waited in the tiring-house for his cue to run to the area near where the theater's flag flew, high above the stage. Since there were no artificial lights to dim and no stage curtain to lift, the trumpet calls were the audience's only sign that the play was about to begin.

Generally, the characters' entrance, through one of the tiring-house doors or openings, was announced with such lines of dialogue as "My lady comes" or "Who comes here?" In addition to directing attention to an incoming actor or actors, these lines filled a potentially awkward pause in the course of the play, providing the time needed for an actor to get into position onstage. Playwrights similarly gave actors lines to allow time for their movement across the vast platform to exit the scene. For example, when a character in act 4, scene 14, of Shakespeare's *Antony and Cleopatra* shouts, "To the monument!"[30] he is signaling his exit—and also the end of a scene. Such exit lines functioned in the same way as dropping a curtain in a theater does in plays written today.

The Globe did not use sets, so playwrights also used dialogue to locate scenes. For example, Shakespeare has Rosalind, his heroine in *As You Like It,* specify, "Well, this is the forest of Arden."[31] A small tree or two might have been brought out onstage to symbolize an entire forest, but otherwise, Rosalind's remark was the audience's only clue that the action of the play was then unfolding in the woods.

This "unlocalized" nature of the Globe's stage allowed it to be thought of as anywhere. As in the classical theater, the *frons scaenae* ("stage wall") could represent some grand palace where kings and queens suffered great tragedies or a private house or inn where characters exposed their foibles in comedies. Of course, the spectators' imaginations needed to be recruited. The speech that opens Shakespeare's *Henry V* reminds the audience of their role in creating the illusions of the theater:

> The vasty fields of France? Or may we cram
> Within this wooden O the very casques [helmets, that is, armies]
> That did affright the air at Agincourt?
> . . . let us . . .
> On your imaginary forces work.
> . . . Think, when we talk of horses, that you see them
> Printing their proud hoofs i' th' receiving earth.[32]

CALLED INTO SERVICE

Although at the Globe no stage curtain was raised to reveal a change of scenery, curtains of some sort—cloth drapes, possibly painted, or even a tapestry, known as an arras—were used in performances. Players, all male in the days of the Globe, rushed about the tiring-house costuming themselves for their various roles (they often played more than one), and curtains drawn across the tiring-house doors conserved heat and eliminated drafts in that space. Also, instead of having to open or close a heavy door, curtains could easily be parted or drawn aside for entrances or exits. In addition, curtains could enhance the drama of a scene—for example, when a character or object previously hidden from view is revealed to the audience. Known as a "discovery," this dramatic device was used from time to time to create surprise or even shock, such as when revealing a

MACBETH FROM THE TIRING-HOUSE

Only bare-boned stage directions appeared in copies of the plays that were published in Elizabethan times, and many of these are suspect since they were added later by editors of Shakespeare's work. Speculation regarding staging at Shakespeare's Globe is therefore a popular sport among theater scholars. Peter Thomson, in his book *Shakespeare's Theatre,* proposed the following commentary on the staging of act 1, scene 7, of the tragedy *Macbeth.*

> The pacing of a play in performance will depend, often uncomfortably, on the exact timing of sound effects and the efficient deployment of properties. . . . The hautboys [wood instruments, like oboes] here, for instance, add to their threatening shrillness a traditional association with feasts and sumptuousness. They both establish and undermine an atmosphere. . . . The servants move in and out of the two stage doors, lit by torches and accompanied by music. Macbeth's lonely entrance breaks the pattern they have established. . . . It is the first time we have seen [Macbeth] alone, and the soliloquy draws us towards that sense of complicity that is a mighty force in our experience of the killing of Duncan [the king, who is a guest at Macbeth's home]. The "overheard" quality of Macbeth's soliloquies invites careful staging. They are not, as Hamlet's are, an open confiding in the audience. It would be interesting to know whether [Richard] Burbage instinctively stopped short of the platform's edge.

dead body. Curtains also supplied hiding places for characters—for instance, when Polonius, spying from behind the arras, is stabbed through it by Hamlet.

Also at times called into service during a play were the stage posts that supported the cover. For example, in Shakespeare's tragedy *Othello,* a post possibly stood in for the "Bulke," or beam of wood, behind which the character of Roderigo hides. Occasionally notices were attached to them, such as the love verses hung by Orlando in another Shakespeare play, *As You Like It.* A post might even have represented a tree, which a character climbed—at least partway, assisted by the molding at its bottom—to avoid pursuers. Characters might also find themselves tied to a post.

Another of the theater's structural elements sometimes enlisted in the action of a play was the tiring-house balcony. In stage directions, a character might appear "aloft" or "above," that is, from a balcony or window or the battlements of a castle. At the Globe, "aloft" was evidently the front area of the tiring-house gallery. Because of the relative difficulty hearing and seeing the actor so situated, action "aloft" was generally limited to the character above interacting briefly with a character or characters below, then descending by way of tiring-house stairs and emerging onto the stage itself. For example, in *The Merchant of Venice* by Shakespeare, a stage direction reads, "Enter Jessica, above, in boy's clothes." Jessica speaks with her lover, Lorenzo, who awaits her below, and throws him down a small chest, after which the directions read, "Exit above," then, seven lines later, "Enter Jessica below."[33]

Possibly creating another level for the action of the play was a kind of porch projecting from above the central opening in the tiring-house facade. The roof of this structure apparently served as the floor of a small stage, allowing for more action than did the gallery. Pushed forward onto the Globe's platform when needed and curtained below to direct the audience's attention to the roof area, it provided a fairly good view of the actors atop it. Such a raised porch may have served as the monument in *Antony and Cleopatra*, upon which the character of Antony is lifted to join Cleopatra, attended there by her maids.

PLENTY OF PROPS

Big set pieces, such as Cleopatra's monument, may have been erected on stage before the start of the play to avoid disrupting the pace of the drama. However, tents, mentioned particularly in battle scenes, may have been set up during the play as part of the action on the battlefield. Shakespeare's *Richard III*, for example, opens with the king's command, "Here pitch our tent, even here in Bosworth field"—and six lines later the order, "Up with my tent."[34]

A common stage direction during the course of a play was for certain large props to be "thrust out"—presumably through the tiring-house's central curtained opening—including thrones, tombs, and tables complete with plaster molds of fruit and fish. Carried onto the stage during plays were such items as rocks, hedges, a "magic glass," a "Hell mouth," and a prop lion. Stagehands, known as "stage keepers," moved props on and off the platform right before the audience's eyes—calling on viewers to overlook these distractions.

Of course, actors themselves brought props onto the stage that were appropriate to their character in a scene. A scepter, for example, identified the actor who held it as a king or queen. At other times, hand props helped establish in a time- (and money-) saving way what occurred in a scene offstage. For instance, stage directions in a play called *Woodstock* instruct the actors to enter with napkins on their arms and knives in their fists, suggesting they had been interrupted at their meal; it is later revealed that an attempt had been made to poison them at a banquet.

Props such as jeweled crowns, brightly colored banners, and flashing swords certainly added to the visual display of processions and battle scenes. Further contributing to the visual excitement of the play was the blood and gore often seen to spill out of characters. In stage fights, a player might hide a pig's bladder under his jacket that would be pierced with a sword, causing the blood in the bladder to spout from the "wound." Scenes of execution were even staged in which the insides of animals bought from slaughterhouses were scooped out of the "victims" and shown to spectators, just as real-life executioners removed the organs of their real-life victims and displayed them to crowds of onlookers. This offered a kind of brutal entertainment as well as a warning of the dire consequences of treasonous acts.

SPECIAL EFFECTS

Clearly, the Globe did not shy away from spectacle. Besides its store of varied and colorful props, the theater was well equipped to create the late-sixteenth- and early-seventeenth-century equivalents of special effects. For example, in Shakespeare's *Macbeth*, the witch's cauldron apparently rose up from below the stage trap and sank down again. During *Hamlet*, a coffin was lowered into the trap (as into a recently dug grave), followed by two players jumping onto it. The trap therefore must have measured at least seven-and-a-half or even eight feet long—long enough for a coffin to be placed in it without tilting—and must have been wide enough to accommodate two people. When descending into it using stairs or a ladder, actors would have had to duck sideways to avoid a bump on the head as the trap fell. Rectangular in shape, the trap had its long axis parallel to the front of the stage to enable actors, descending or ascending, to be in view of most of the audience.

Housed over the stage, in the hut, was the gear used for raising and lowering a player over the stage. This old theatrical trick dated back to ancient times: A stage direction in *The Clouds,* by fourth-century-B.C. playwright Aristophanes, for example, reads, "The machine swings in Socrates in a basket."[35] Known as *deus ex machina* (literally, god from a machine), the effect introduced a god using a crane over the stage; the god would then intervene in the action of the play. At the Globe, the hoist, or suspension mechanism, was a rope wound around a windlass, or reel, to make it easier to turn and therefore operate

The property room of the Globe housed the suspension mechanism that was used to lower an actor onto the stage, giving his appearance a "heavenly" effect.

by hand. Tied to the free end of the rope was the seat accommodating the "flying" actor. Surrounding this seat, which usually resembled a bird or a chariot, were "clouds"—that is, billowing folds of cloth—to enhance the "heavenly" effect. Evidence for use of the device appears in Shakespeare's *Cymbeline:* "Jupiter descends in Thunder and Lightning, sitting upon an Eagle; he throws a Thunder-bolt"; then, twenty lines later, Jupiter gives the order, "Mount, Eagle, to my palace crystalline."[36] In *The Prophetess,* written for the Globe in 1622 by John Fletcher and Philip Massinger, the flying seat appeared as a "Throne drawn by Dragons."[37]

Sound effects generally accompanied the workings of the trap and "flying" mechanism. Falling chains and occasionally "hellish musicke" helped create an eerie atmosphere and also disguised the creaking of the trap's boards when it was in operation. The rolling of a cannon ball on a metal sheet signified thunder, and the rumblings of a drum suggested a storm. Lightning was mimicked by fireworks, rigged to run down from the "heavens" on a wire. A large bell was rung to sound an "alarum"—signaling some kind of disturbance, particularly in a battle—while a "chyme of belles" or clock bells marked the passage of time. Cannons were shot off to heighten the drama not only in battle scenes but in scenes of feasting and celebration. Live music, a kind of sound effect emanating from a "musicke-roome" in the gallery above the stage, helped convey the emotion for a particular moment, whether sorrow, longing, or merriment. Instruments such as drums, trumpets, fiddles, and flutes had played a part in public stage performances from earliest times.

In addition to the energetic acting and the pageantry of actors in glittering costumes sweeping across the stage, such aural and visual effects certainly added to the thrill of playgoing. And nearly as much of a thrill as watching a play at the Globe was producing one. The exploits of the theater's actor-owners, with tension and turmoil arising from the ups and downs of fortune, often matched the drama onstage. Plying their trade at a time of economic opportunity, theater folk in the Elizabethan period nevertheless depended for their livelihood on unpredictable forces: from the clash of politics to the whim of fashion to the outbreak of disease. Those who called the Globe their theatrical home continually faced uncertainty.

DEBITS AND CREDITS

By building and outfitting their own playhouse, the Globe's actor-owners clearly demonstrated the enterprising spirit that animated the Elizabethan Age. They were entrepreneurs, trailblazing a new kind of theatrical management.

Under immense pressure to succeed at their pioneering venture, which plays did the Chamberlain's Men present during the Globe's opening season? Elizabethan scholar Peter Thomson speculates what the theater's bill included for the year 1599:

> The Chamberlain's Men would have wanted to get the right play for the grand opening. . . . A play by Shakespeare was the likeliest choice, perhaps the festive comedy of *As You Like It,* whose very title is an advertising promise. . . . Shakespeare had been occupied over the summer with the writing of *Julius Caesar* . . . there is no doubt that Shakespeare took particular pains over its composition. It is a tightly controlled piece, restricted in its imagery and even in vocabulary, as though put together with a consciousness of the weight it must carry.
>
> *As You Like It* and *Julius Caesar* were, in their distinct ways, popular. The other surviving play from the 1599 repertoire was an altogether riskier affair. . . . *Every Man out of His Humour,* the play [by Ben Jonson] sold to the Chamberlain's Men . . . , includes a wicked portrait of [rival playwright John] Marston . . . together with one of [another rival playwright Thomas] Dekker. . . . *Every Man out of His Humour* was an extraordinarily bold choice for a company striving to establish its image in new surroundings. . . . Controversy, they must have calculated, is good publicity.[38]

RISK TAKING

The Globe's actor-managers were risk takers in more ways than one. When the Globe opened, it was still at the heart of a lawsuit by the Burbages' former landlord, Gyles Allen. Not until three years later, in 1602, would there be an end to the attacks Allen mounted against the Burbages in London's courts.

Entering into a fray between feuding playwrights and continuing legal battles with Gyles Allen were not the only controversies to embroil the new playhouse. Just about a year and a half after its opening, the Globe was caught up in political scandal. In February 1601, friends of Robert Devereaux, the earl of Essex, arrived at the playhouse and, according to the testimony of a member of the company, "spoke to some of the players in the presence of this Examinate to have the play of the deposing and killing of King Richard the Second to be played the Saturday next, promising to get them xls. [40 shillings] more than their ordinary to play it."[39] The earl had been a favorite of Queen Elizabeth I but had been under house arrest the year before, and he remained banned at court. Convinced that Queen Elizabeth needed saving from the clutches of a corrupt court, Essex hoped that performing *Richard II* would raise awareness of what he saw as Elizabeth's plight.

Robert Devereaux, the earl of Essex, was convinced that Queen Elizabeth was in danger from members of a corrupt court.

On February 7, Shakespeare's *Richard II*, a play about an English monarch forced to renounce the throne, was presented at the Globe. The next morning, Essex and a couple hundred followers rode through London's streets, shouting that the Crown of England had been "sold" to a foreign power. Failing to arouse support, the unfortunate earl was captured and sentenced to die as a traitor.

Why the Globe's players risked implication in Essex's rebellion by presenting just the day before such a politically explosive play as *Richard II*, with its appeal to seditious feelings, remains a mystery. Possibly, as a noted patron of poets, the earl was friendly with Shakespeare. In any event, the company, including Shakespeare as the play's author, somehow avoided being thrown into prison. In fact, records confirm that the queen did not withdraw their invitation to perform at court on February 24, the day before Essex's beheading.

"FOR THE RECREATION OF OUR LOVING SUBJECTS"

Queen Elizabeth was certainly a great lover of plays. Her death in March 1603 left London's theatrical community holding its breath in anticipation. Would her successor be as supportive of theater? Royal support was vital not only for the fashionability of playgoing but also, in the face of London's hostile government leaders, for its very existence. Fortunately for those in the theatrical world, England's new ruler, James I, was an avid playgoer. Known as King James VI of Scotland before ascending the English throne, James had championed actors against attacks by Scotland's church, even dismissing a decree by the nation's clergy that "none should resort to these profane comedies."[40]

James I, Queen Elizabeth's successor, was an avid theatergoer himself and appointed the Chamberlain's Men to be his own royal players. They were therefore renamed the King's Men.

James's ascension to England's throne proved particularly fortunate for the Chamberlain's Men. At the very beginning of his reign, James I appointed them to be his own royal players. Undergoing a name change to reflect this fact, the company was known as the King's Men following the issuance of their new letters of patent, dated May 19, 1603:

> Know ye that We of our special grace, certain knowledge, & mere motion have licensed and authorized . . . these our Servants . . . to use and exercise the Art and faculty of playing Comedies, Tragedies, histories, Enterludes, morals, pastorals, Stage-plays, and Such others . . . as well for the recreation of our loving Subjects, as for our Solace and pleasure when we shall think good to see them.[41]

Sponsorship by the king—and the protection it promised—was a distinct advantage for the company. It meant greater stability for them, as well as greater prestige. Following James's death, a new patent would be issued for the King's Men on June 24, 1625, as Charles I inherited not only the throne but also the royal acting troupe.

The choice of Burbage and company for royal favor suggests they were the leading players of the day. However, they faced a rival: the Lord Admiral's Men, under the leadership of the popular actor Edward Alleyn. Not surprisingly, Alleyn's company was financed by his father-in-law, Philip Henslowe, one of London theater's great impresarios. The rivalry between the two groups heated up in the winter of 1597–1598, when authorities legally restricted the number of London acting companies to two: the (then) Lord Chamberlain's Men and the Lord Admiral's Men.

Their rivalry is evidenced in Henslowe's construction, just a year after the Globe was built, of the Fortune playhouse for use by the Lord Admiral's Men. The wording of Henslowe and Alleyn's contract with Peter Streete, who was also master carpenter for the Globe, illustrates the competition between the two groups. Throughout, Streete is directed to fashion some feature or other to be like its counterpart at the Globe, summarizing, "And the said house and other things beforementioned to be made & done to be in all other contritivions, conveyances, fashions, thing and things effected, finished and done according to the manner and fashion of the said house called the Globe."[42]

KING JAMES I

When Elizabeth I died in 1603, the Crown passed peaceably to the king of Scotland, James VI, Elizabeth's closest relative. Fortunately for Burbage and company, and their Globe playhouse, the new ruler loved theater. In fact, despite the opposition of his dour ministers in Scotland, he succeeded in legalizing plays in his native country. Within a mere ten days after arriving in London, James took on the sponsorship of its leading acting troupe, the Chamberlain's Men, which promptly became known as the King's Men.

The chief playwright for the troupe was William Shakespeare. Shakespeare's famous tragedy *Macbeth* was written in response to a handwritten note from James requesting a play about Scotland. Some scholars claim that *Macbeth* was written to flatter James, citing as evidence that the play portrays his lineage in a positive light and that its plot concerns ghosts and witches, subject matter that was of interest to the king.

Edward Alleyn, leader of the Lord Admiral's Men.

PROFIT SHARING

Rivalry from the outside was just one of the problems confronting the Globe. The theater's survival was also prey to the whims of its own investors. The Globe's resident company suffered a betrayal of sorts when Will Kempe abruptly quit soon after the theater's opening. Whatever his reasons, Kempe's desertion dealt a severe blow to the players' launching their new venture. They had lost not only their most crowd-pleasing comedian but also one of their partners in financial liability.

Kempe was one of the original investors in the Globe, along with the Burbage brothers—Richard and Cuthbert—and Shakespeare, Augustine Phillips, Thomas Pope, and John Heminge. Their investment scheme was an innovative one, since no other playhouse at the time was owned by its principal players. The arrangement guaranteed them a permanent home and also saved them the cost of rent. They were housekeepers, or theater owners and managers, as well as sharers. (Sharers formed the core of principal actors of a company who each held "shares" of stock in the company and divided up its profits.) The names of the sharers appeared in the company's patent, identifying them as "patented members." Shakespeare—earning about £55 annually from his share—amassed enough money over the years to buy property in his hometown of Stratford, at a time when playwrights were rarely rich.

Very likely, the players' financial interest in their own theater contributed to the company's success. Free of the need to pay rent, the sharers of the Globe, as a whole as well as individually, enjoyed a financial advantage over sharers of other companies. The company's survival may have depended in part on this advantage. Every other London troupe was either splitting up at the time or reorganizing under a different name. So strong was the bond uniting the Globe's sharers that they were apparently willing to overlook the fact that some profited more than others. The Burbages actually owned half the shares, while the remaining shares were divided among Shakespeare, Phillips, Pope, Heminge, and, before his defection, Kempe. Though potentially a cause of conflict, the skewing of profits to the benefit of the Burbages does not seem to have disrupted the partnership.

RICHARD BURBAGE

The most famous actor of his day, Richard Burbage originated the starring roles of Hamlet, Macbeth, Richard III, Othello, and King Lear. Some scholars speculate that Burbage's talent may have inspired Shakespeare to create the complex and challenging parts for actors that he did. Shakespeare's respect and admiration for the interpreter of his greatest characters is suggested by the fact that, when he died, he left Burbage a ring as a remembrance of their friendship. Burbage's command of the stage is even more impressive considering his short, heavyset build—he obviously lacked the good looks that today are expected of Hollywood idols.

Richard Burbage starred in many of Shakespeare's plays, originating roles such as Hamlet, Macbeth, and King Lear.

Having grown up in a theatrical family—his father, James, was the owner and manager of the Theatre—Burbage was already a well-known actor by the time he was twenty. He apparently continued to perform up to his death in 1619, at about age fifty. His passing caused public grief. Reportedly, the mourning was greater for him than for England's then-queen, Anne. In volume 4 of *The* Revels *History of Drama in English*, Gerald Eades Bentley quotes playwright Thomas Middleton: "To the people, Dick Burbage was their mortal god on earth." Fittingly, because his life was so intertwined with theater, the epitaph on his gravestone reads, "Exit Burbage."

The written will of one member reveals how closely knit the Globe's resident company was. Augustine Phillips left 20 shilling gold pieces to five of his fellow shareholders, with a special gift of silver bowls to both John Heminge and Richard Burbage. He also willed £5 to be divided among the hired men of the company. These were actors who played minor roles, as well as others instrumental in running the theater, such as the wardrobe master and stage keepers. Because they invested no capital in the theater, they received no share in the profits and instead, as "hired men," were paid weekly wages. Richard Cowley, a hired man who eventually became a sharer in the company, further demonstrated the family feeling among the troupe by naming two of his sons after the Burbage brothers.

EARNINGS AND EXPENSES

Loyalty aside, the Globe profited its investors. For a performance of the phenomenally successful play *A Game at Chesse*, for example, receipts at the Globe totaled £100. Over a period of five years during summer performances, records show that, on average, the King's Men as a company took in £6, 13 shillings, and 8 pence a day.

From these earnings, the wages of the theater's hired men and other day-to-day expenses were paid. These amounted to about £3 a day, or £900 to £1,000 a year, not including the cost of costumes and writers' fees. Other expenses probably included the purchase of a boat, possibly 70 shillings, for transporting costumes and props across the Thames, and timber and paint when repairs to the theater were necessary. Another expense was the licensing fee paid to the Crown for permission to perform plays. In 1599, the year the Globe opened, this fee rose from 10 shillings a week to £3—six times as much—per month.

Because of the open-air design of the Globe, plays may not have been performed there year-round. During London's colder months, the Globe apparently hosted entertainment besides plays—particularly after 1608, when the King's Men took up winter residence at the Blackfriars, an indoor playhouse. It is unlikely that Burbage and company would have allowed the Globe to remain empty when they could profit from renting it for other purposes, such as performances by rope dancers, fencers, and "vaulters." There is evidence, for example, of a "Dutch vaulter"—an athlete of some kind, probably a pole vaulter—at

APPRENTICES

Aspiring actors in the days of the Globe—there were no aspiring actresses, as women appearing onstage would have shocked audiences—did not attend drama schools. Instead they learned their craft by being apprenticed to actors who had already established themselves in the profession. Apprentices were working members of an acting troupe, the lowest ranked, and relatively well paid at 3 shillings a week. Beginning their apprenticeship at about the age of ten, they rigorously trained to develop powerful, agile bodies and clear, strong voices. Their studies included singing, dancing, and possibly acrobatics. Staged battles and hand-to-hand combat were popular with playgoers, so apprentices learned to take falls without damaging themselves or their expensive costumes. They were also taught to be skilled with the sword and dagger.

While an apprentice studied and worked in the theater, he lived in the home of his master. Following the system of other trades, veteran actors fed and housed as well as guided the education of their apprentices, treating them as members of their own family.

the Globe in February 1630. Evidence also exists of a match in February 1603 between two famed fencers at a Bankside theater, possibly the Globe, that ended suddenly when one stabbed the other "so far in the brain at the eye"[43] that he died instantly.

To some extent, expenses were offset by income from food and drink concessions that operated before and during performances. At the Globe, vendors moved about the audience, selling apples or oranges or servings of beer. In addition, the property the Globe's investors leased from the Brend family was large enough to include a tap house, or pub—attested to by sharers' papers in 1635 showing it to be in the householders' possession. Although the Globe was theirs rent-free—since they owned it—the property it stood on, belonging to whoever might be the current Sir Brend, was not. The rent the Globe's householders paid to that gentleman was partially met by subletting the tap house, possibly at £20 or £30 a year. This extra income was always welcome as a hedge against the periods of financial hardship that would have otherwise threatened the livelihood of players and theater owners.

"BROUGHT INTO DANGER OF GOD'S WRATH"

Losses naturally resulted when authorities ordered theaters to temporarily close their doors to the public. Restrictions on performances were in some cases religious. For example, during Lent, the Christian period of fasting that begins forty days before Easter, attendance at playhouses was forbidden. If they could afford to, theater managers foiled this ban by paying church authorities for the privilege of presenting plays during the Lenten period. The ban remained in force without exception, though, on Wednesdays and Thursdays, which were known as sermon days, and during Holy Week, between Palm Sunday and Easter Sunday. Laws against performing plays on other Sundays were often ignored.

Authorities were more effective in keeping playhouses shut down during periodic outbreaks of the bubonic plague. Known

When the Black Death struck London, gathering places such as playhouses were shut down in hopes of slowing the spread of the epidemic.

as the Black Death, the disease first entered London in 1348, and the plague continued to surface from time to time for centuries. Epidemics could be devastating. In a single year, 1592, the plague wiped out 10 percent of London's population. City officials had observed that quarantines kept the death rate down. They therefore ordered that public gathering places, including playhouses, close when reported deaths reached forty in a week.

From their pulpits, Puritan preachers thundered that the plague was punishment for sinful playgoing, the playgoing population of London being "brought into danger of God's wrath, and their own condemnation, in as much as they are partakers of the sins of the Players and of the Plays in approving them."[44] Blaming the plague on theatergoing was, of course, not medically valid. Nevertheless, packing large groups of people together in close quarters—as at Elizabethan playhouses—can contribute to the spread of infectious disease. In addition, the thatched roofs of the public playhouses attracted rats, and the plague, it is now known, was carried by rat fleas. So closing the theaters during outbreaks of the plague may well have saved some lives.

"OF OUR FREE GIFT AND BOUNTY"

Playhouses were often closed down for months at a time; in 1630, the closing order issued on April 17 was not lifted until November 12. The effect on the actor's morale is suggested by a character in Lording Barry's *Ram Alley*, who admits shrinking at the sight of an officer "almost as much as a new Player does at a plague bill certifying forty"[45]—that is, a notice that deaths that week had exceeded the limit of forty.

Early in September 1637, after nearly sixteen months of a ban on plays, the King's Men petitioned for permission to perform in the city of Michaelmas on September 29: "His Majesty's Servants ye Players, having, by reason of the Infection of the Plague in and near London, been for a long time restrained and having now spent what they got in many years before and so not able any longer to subsist and maintain their families did by their Petition to his Majesty: most humbly desire leave to be now at liberty to use their quality." Permission was granted, with one condition: "if there be no considerable increase of the sickness, nor that there die more than died last week."[46] With the records showing an increase of five deaths over the preceding weeks, the luckless players remained idle on Michaelmas, though theaters were allowed to reopen within a few days, on October 2.

To help offset financial loss during plague years, acting companies reluctantly abandoned their playhouses in the city and set out to perform in towns and villages in the outlying countryside. In the summer of 1606, for example, the itinerary of the King's Men included Marlborough, Oxford, Leicester, Dover, and Maidstone. On the road, however, costs—including risk of highway robbery—were high, and profits few. In the provinces, audiences were much smaller than in London, if an audience could be gathered at all. Many villagers were suspicious of professional actors and avoided encouraging their presence by attending plays.

Twice, in 1603 and again in 1609, King James bestowed £30 on his financially strapped company. His successor, Charles I, also granted his players funds—in 1625, 1630, and 1636, even upping the amount: "We are graciously pleased, in regard of their great hindrance *of late received* . . . to bestow upon them the sum of one hundred pounds . . . as of our free gift and bounty, without any . . . charge to be set upon . . . them."[47]

"SUNDRY SLAUGHTERS AND MAYHEMMINGS"

While King James and King Charles freely gave of their bounty, there were those who freely took of the bounty offered by theaters such as the Globe. Pickpockets are known to have moved among the jostling crowds at playhouses. Known as cutpurses, they "cut" the straps of hanging "purses" where people of the period kept their money; at the time clothes did not have sewn-in pockets.

The audience's tendency to become rowdy at times was also a concern. On one occasion, authorities canceled the performance of a play at the Globe on the suspicion of riot. A report claimed "that on Thursday next, divers loose and Idle persons, some Sailors, and other, have appointed to meet at the Play-house called the Globe, to see a Play (as is pretended) but their end is thereby to disguise some . . . Riotous action."[48] London officials roundly condemned "the inordinate haunting of great multitudes of people, specially youth, to plays," where they were prey to robberies "by picking and cutting of purses" and "besides that also sundry slaughters and mayhemmings . . . by ruins of Scaffolds, Frames and Stages, and by engines, weapons and powder used in plays."[49]

The Globe did, in fact, fall victim to "powder" one summer day. On June 29, 1613, the theater presented a new play about Henry VIII, titled *All Is True*. To dramatically announce the arrival of King Henry, a cannon was fired, probably from the "attic" above the stage. Some wadding from the barrel of the cannon landed on the roof, which then started to smolder. Sir Henry Wotton, in a letter to his nephew four days later, described what happened next: "Being thought at first but an idle smoke, and [the audience's] eyes more attentive to the show, it kindled inwardly, and ran around like a train, consuming within less than an hour the whole house to the very grounds."[50] Because the Globe, other than its brick foundation, was made entirely of timber, lath, and plaster, once the fire took hold, stopping it was nearly impossible.

The audience's tendency to become rowdy sometimes caused authorities to cancel performances.

Remarkably, in a theater filled with people, not a single life was lost. "Only one man," stated Sir Wotton, "had his breeches set on fire, that would perhaps have broiled him, if he had not by the benefit of a provident wit, put it out with bottle ale."[51] The day after the fire—the first in the history of Elizabethan playhouses—ballads were circulated, including "The Sudden Burning of the 'Globe' on the Bankside in the Play Time on Saint Peters Day Last 1613" and "A Doleful Ballad on the General Overthrow of the Famous Theater on the Bankside, called the 'Globe.'" Poems lamenting the disaster followed, including the anonymous "Sonnet Upon the Pitiful Burning of the Globe Playhouse in London," and Ben Jonson's often quoted poem "An Execration upon *Vulcan.*" "See the worlds Ruins!"[52] Jonson proclaimed—and some may have wondered if they would see its like again.

THE COMEBACK

By the summer following the fire, the Globe was back in operation. On June 30, 1614, a contemporary, John Chamberlain, wrote, "Indeed I hear much speech of this new play-house, which is said to be the fairest that ever was in England."[53]

The speed with which the Globe was rebuilt was helped by the fact that its original piles and foundation walls had survived the fire that destroyed the rest of the playhouse. The building of the second Globe on the foundation of the first is attested to by a 1634 document surveying new (and at the time illegal) building in the city, exempting "The Globe playhouse near Maid lane . . . built with timber, about 20 years past, upon an old foundation."[54]

The total cost of reconstruction was £1,400, which was more than twice the amount spent to build the original Globe. Fortunately, the owners had plenty of money. In fact, the group included some of London's wealthiest actors, many of them having profited from being partners in constructing and operating the first Globe playhouse on the Bankside.

"IN FAR FAIRER MANNER"

Although the second Globe was probably no larger than its predecessor, the playhouse apparently did boast some improvements. Edmond Howes, writing in 1615, claims that it "was new builded in far fairer manner than before."[55] Howes probably meant that it displayed more ornamentation, that is, more carvings and decorative touches on the tiring-house facade. Reportedly displayed on the facade—or, possibly, outside the theater itself—was a carving of the mythological character Atlas holding up a globe, underneath it written in Latin the line from Shakespeare's *As You Like It:* "All the world's a stage."

As greater assurance to life and property, the first Globe's humble thatched roof was replaced with one of tile. Tile, as a fired clay material, was less flammable than thatching. However, it was also less water-resistant. Gutters therefore were installed to direct rain off the roof. In addition, modern-day theater designer C. Walter Hodges supposes that, with advancements in theater building in the dozen or so years between the construction of the first Globe and the second, the area underneath the stage of the newer playhouse would have been masked with timber boards, rather than with cloth, which is a flimsier material.

All in all, improvements to the Globe inspired the poet John Taylor to declare,

> As Gold is better that's in fire tried,
> So the bankside Globe that late was burn'd:
> For where before it had a thatched hide,
> Now to a stately Theater is turn'd
> Which is an Emblem, that great things are won
> By those that dare through greatest dangers run.[56]

TOPPING THE THEATER

Proper to a grander theater, the second Globe's stage was increased to extend the full width of the yard to the galleries on either side. This expansion reflected the playhouse's enlarged superstructure—including hut area and stage cover—above. Evidently, the superstructure covered almost half the yard. Thus early-arriving groundlings may have enjoyed overhead shelter that they lacked before.

Also as a result of the expansion, the increased hut area provided more storage space for the company's costumes and props. The area was increased by adding to the number of huts rather than to the size of a single hut, because two large huts side by side balanced the enlarged superstructure better than a single, enormous one would.

Nestled between these twin gables, or peaks, was a domed, turretlike structure about eight feet across. This cupola served to let in extra light. It would have allowed additional daylight into the interior of the superstructure as well as onto the back parts of the stage and the tiring-house facade. The additional light was needed because the more expansive superstructure would have greatly darkened those areas, particularly on the gloomier days of the year.

RE-RIGGING AN EFFECT

The enlargement of the superstructure also required a re-rigging of the Globe's flying mechanism. No longer was a direct drop to

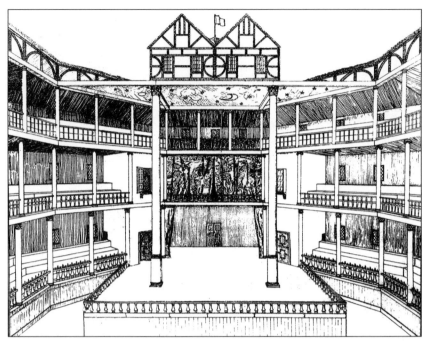

When rebuilding the Globe, the superstructure was expanded, providing shelter for early-arriving groundlings.

the stage from overhead possible. A launching platform with a catwalk, or narrow walkway, built centrally into the interior of the superstructure would have blocked light from the cupola.

Instead, room for the necessary winding gear—consisting of a barrel-like windlass and hoisting ropes—as well as for the actor to be prepared in the flying seat, was likely found above the tiring-house, toward the back of the huge, soaring superstructure. Preparation for the effect would have taken place behind a screen painted with clouds and stars, placed above the tiring-house facade.

The effect itself was now managed by a simple, fourteen- to fifteen-foot crane hinged to the launching platform. A system of ropes and pulleys operated the crane. Hanging by a pair of long ropes that ran back around the pulleys, the seat was swung forward by the crane until it hung over the stage. At the same time, the windlass was released, allowing the ropes carrying the seat to run out so that it—and the actor riding in it—dropped gently toward the stage. With practice, the entire maneuver could have been managed in a single, relatively smooth movement.

SUPERSIZING THE SUPERSTRUCTURE

The newly constructed superstructure would have resembled an open, hollow shell, so those standing on the stage looking up could see into its arched framework. The timbers providing structural support were not long enough to reach all the way across. Instead, a parallel series of paired beams extended from opposite sides into the open space between, each beam reinforced by a brace—a timber that arched from a vertical post to shore up the beam from underneath.

This series of beams, known as hammer beams, relied on balance as well as wooden pegs and joinery to hold together—nothing more. In other words, the superstructure's hammer-beam design allowed it to be self-supporting so that supporting posts would not be necessary. That was fortunate for the audience, since the expansion of the superstructure would have required either more or heavier posts than those placed on the stage to support the superstructure of the first Globe, which would have seriously interfered with the audience's view of the play. Its self-supporting roof, then, greatly benefited the new theater's sight lines.

The King's Men may have hit upon the idea of a self-supporting superstructure for their rebuilt theater—effectively banishing posts from the stage—based on their experience performing at the Blackfriars. A private, indoor playhouse also owned by the Burbage brothers, the Blackfriars boasted a hammer-beam roof. Richard and Cuthbert Burbage might well have taken their builder to the Blackfriars and asked him to construct something similar to overarch the stage and tiring-house of the new Globe.

PUBLIC VERSUS PRIVATE

Private, indoor theaters like the Blackfriars were increasingly attracting a well-to-do audience, who preferred the comparative comfort and exclusiveness of these playhouses to open-air public playhouses like the Globe. Private playhouses also offered the novelty of boys performing the plays, at least until 1608, when boys' companies went out of fashion. The boys' companies, which evolved out of boys' school choirs, performed infrequently compared with adult players, and they presented plays—at least in principle—to demonstrate the fruits of their education, rather than for profit. Performances by boy players, therefore, were aimed at audiences well educated enough to appreciate less spectacular and more subtle fare—and wealthy enough to pay for the privilege.

As a result, London theater began dividing along class lines, and private playhouses became linked with sophistication and public playhouses with broad humor, action, and show. James Shirley's *Prologue at the Globe to his Comedy call'd* The doubtfull Heire, *which should have been presented at the Black-Friers* makes this distinction clear:

> Gentlemen, I am onely sent to say,
> Our Author did not calculate this Play,
> For this Meridian; the Bank-side he knowes,
> Is far more skillful at the ebbes and flowes
> Of Water than of Wit; He did not mean
> For the elevation of your Poles this Scene,
> No shews, no frisk, and what you most delight in,
> (Grave understanders) here's no Target fighting
> Upon the Stage, all work for Cutlers barrd,
> No Bawd'ry, nor no Ballads; this goes hard,
> The wit is clean, and (what affects you not)
> Without impossibilities the plot;
> No Clown, no squibs, no Divvell's in't; oh now
> You Squirrels that want nuts, what will ye do?
> Pray do not crack the benches, and we may
> Hereafter fit your plats with a Play.
> But you that can contract your selves, and sit
> As you were now in the Black-Friers pit,
> And will not deaf us with lewd noise, or tongues,
> Because we have no heart to break our lungs,
> Will pardon our vast Scene, and not disgrace
> This Play, meant for your persons, not the place.[57]

A public theater "hijacking" a play intended for the private stage was nothing new. In 1606, a play originally written for a boys' company was presented at the Globe: John Marston's *The Malcontent*. In their defense, the Globe's players claimed that a boys' company had itself "stolen" a public theater play, probably *The Spanish Tragedy* by Thomas Kyd, which was wildly popular in its day. In any case, additional material needed to be written for the version of *The Malcontent* performed at the Globe. Plays intended for indoor playhouses were shorter than

THE WAR OF THE THEATERS

Early in the seventeenth century, intense competition between playwrights, as well as between boys' companies at private theaters and adult actors at public playhouses like the Globe, sparked what became known as the Poetomachia, or War of the Theaters. At the time, almost every major English playwright was writing for the boy players—except Shakespeare, who, as a shareholder, had a stake in his own company's success at the Globe.

The Globe's players were drawn into the battle in 1601 when, at the Blackfriars, the Children of the Chapel performed Ben Jonson's *Poetaster*. This play not only continued Jonson's attacks on rival playwrights John Marston and Thomas Dekker but also lampooned the Chamberlain's Men—possibly in retaliation over the failure of Jonson's *Every Man Out of His Humour* at the Globe. The Chamberlain's Men fought back with a performance at the Globe of Dekker's *Satiromastix*, which mocked Jonson's rumored behavior at playhouses: sitting in the gallery, making faces, and striding onstage following a performance of one of his plays—all to draw attention to himself.

Hostilities lasted about a year. Afterward, no one appears to have held grudges. Jonson was soon writing again for the Globe. Not only that but, a decade later, three boy actors with major roles in *Poetaster* joined the Globe's players.

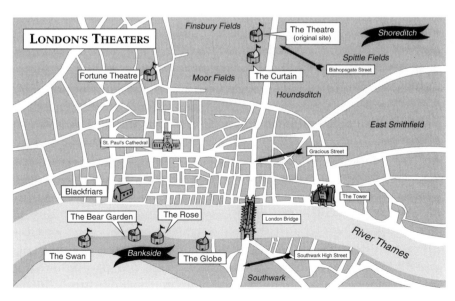

those for open-air theaters, to allow for musical interludes during pauses when the candles providing the lighting were replaced.

Tensions aroused by rivalries had longer-lasting results for the Globe and its players than reworking individual plays, however. Competition between public and private theaters would cause irreversible changes in the relationship between the King's Men and their playhouse on the Bankside.

ECLIPSE

By 1616, because the Blackfriars attracted a "higher class" audience—and also outperformed the Globe financially—it supplanted the Globe as the principal playhouse of the King's Men. Shakespeare's later plays all debuted at the Blackfriars rather than at the Globe.

Still, the company continued performing at the Globe because it remained profitable for them to do so. Though the admission charge at the Blackfriars was much higher—six times the fee at the Globe—its capacity was much less. In general, year-round performance at the Blackfriars was not cost-effective. In the summertime, its audience fled London. They packed off to country homes, or, in the case of the students at the Inns of Court—a sort of unofficial law school—they went home on vacation to family estates.

So, although its profits averaged barely half those of the Blackfriars, the Globe remained of enough value to the company that the King's Men took the time to rebuild it when it burned down. After all, in 1613, as the fire raged at the Globe, the company had become well established at the Blackfriars.

POWER PLAYS

As the seventeenth century wore on, the playhouses reflected not only the class divisions of London society, based on the different kinds of audiences that frequented private as opposed to public theaters, but also the increasing divisiveness of political factions threatening the nation's peace. Opening at the Globe on August 6, 1624, Thomas Middleton's *Game at Chesse* viciously attacked King James's foreign policy. Drawing on anti-Spanish feeling among the public, the play was a hit. How Middleton's inflammatory manuscript got licensed by the master of revels in the first place is a question that remains unanswered. In any case, the play was ordered to close after a wildly successful run—the Globe was rumored to have amassed £1,500 in admissions. Consequently, the players were called before the Privy Council and a warrant posted for Middleton's arrest.

Middleton managed to disappear, and the company was reprimanded and forbidden to perform until further notice. Subsequently, a letter to the council expressed the king's will:

> That his Majesty: now Conceives ye punishment if not satisfactory for all their Insolency, yet such, as since it stops ye Current of their poor livelihood and maintenance without much prejudice they cannot longer undergo. In commiseration therefore of those his poor servants, his Majesty: would have . . . that they shall act as before; As for this of ye Game and Chesse, that it be not only antiquated and silenced but ye Players bound as formerly they were, and in that point only never to Act it again.[58]

Thomas Middleton's Game at Chesse *sparked controversy over King James's foreign policy and was ordered to close.*

The influence of politics on English theater increased after about 1629, with James's successor, Charles I, seeking to assert absolute personal rule. In the summer of 1638, the King's Men again endured royal censorship. *The King and the Subject,* by Phillip Messinger, fell into the hands of the king himself, "who reading over the play . . . set his mark upon the place with his own hand, and in these words: 'This is too insolent, and to be changed,'"[59] according to the records of the master of revels.

In the 1640s, attempts to censor theater in England intensified. Puritan preachers had been railing against the playhouses since the 1570s, when John Stockwood thundered, "Will not a filthy play, with the blast of a trumpet, sooner call thither a thousand, than an hour's tolling of a Bell, bring to the Sermon a hundred?"[60] Political and religious pressures on theatergoing joined forces as the Puritan faction increasingly dominated the English

CENSORSHIP

As an outlet for political and social criticism and also as an occasion for crowds to gather (other than to witness executions), plays were suspected of influencing public opinion and behavior. In response to royal concerns, the post of master of revels was formally established. An official of the royal government, the master of revels licensed and censored plays and supervised playhouses. Initially, his job was to shield citizens from plays promoting sedition or incitement to riot and revolution. And all new plays had to pass his inspection before being produced.

In a time of growing political strain, beginning in 1630, satirical remarks about courtiers and the use of profane language were also being censored by the master of revels. The king himself was more forgiving when it came to defining profanity; he intervened occasionally to blunt the censor's pen. The master of revels also cracked down on actors' attempts to avoid his censure by performing old plays, already licensed, as a way of commenting on contemporary situations. In 1639, for example, players at the Fortune were fined £1,000 for allegedly reviving a play, *The Cardinal's Conspiracy*, in an effort to mock current practices of the Church of England.

Parliament. Finally, on February 4, 1642, *The True Diurnal Occurrences* records, "there was a great complaint made against the Play-houses, and a motion made for the suppressing of them."[61]

"THESE VERY HARD CONDITIONS"

The last official mention of the King's Men is the granting of a license for their performance of a Shirley play, *The Sisters*, on April 26, 1642. The play's prologue suggests the glum outlook of the theater world at the time:

> Our Poet thinks the whole Town is not well,
> Has took some Physick lately, and for fear
> Of catching cold dares not salute this Ayr
> . . . and a Play
> Though ne'r so new, will starve the second day:
> Upon these very hard conditions.[62]

Just five months later, almost immediately after the outbreak of civil war pitting the king, Charles I, against Parliament, the playhouses were ordered closed. On September 2, 1642, Parliament resolved to

> call for all possible means to appease and avert the Wrath of God appearing in these Judgements; amongst which, Fasting and Prayer having been often tried to be very effectual, have been lately, and are still enjoined; and whereas public Sports do not well agree with public Calamities, nor public Stage-plays with the Seasons of Humiliation, this being an Exercise of sad and pious solemnity, and the other being Spectacles of pleasure, too commonly expressing lascivious Mirth and Levity: It is therefore thought fit, and Ordained by the Lords and Commons in this Parliament Assembled, that while these sad Causes and set times of Humiliation do continue, public Stage-Plays shall cease, and be forborne.[63]

In defiance of the order, plays continued to be produced here and there. Raids on illegal performances, with actors being carted off to jail, are noted in public records. Perhaps in retaliation against such flouting of the law, an ordinance was passed on February 9, 1648, directing not only the arrest of players but the seizure of receipts, fining of audience members, and demolition of theaters.

FINALE

By the time of the demolition order, however, the Globe had already been torn down. In the dark days following the onset of civil war, the King's Men were forced to dissolve. Costumes and props were sold off, and apparently the Globe itself fell into the hands of Sir Matthew Brend, who leased the company the property on which their playhouse stood. Perhaps ownership of the theater was transferred to Brend in payment of rent that, thanks to the bad times that had befallen the company, was overdue.

In any case, on Monday, April 15, 1644, upon Brend's order, the Globe was demolished to make room for public housing. It was a new era. It had been Sir Matthew's father who had agreed to lease his Bankside property to a band of actors planning a daring enterprise.

CHARLES I

Charles I was a great patron of plays. While he was king, acting companies were summoned to court more frequently than ever before, and he even suggested the plot of James Shirley's *The Gamester.* Nevertheless, his reign ultimately proved to be the undoing of London's playhouses, including the Globe. His insistence on the divine right of kings, claiming supreme government authority, brought about a showdown with Parliament that led to civil war and the closing of the theaters.

Charles I's insistence on the divine right of kings led to a confrontation with Parliament that ultimately resulted in civil war and the closing of the theaters.

In 1641, Charles ordered the arrest of several members of an increasingly Puritan Parliament. He appeared personally with soldiers at the gates to enforce the order, causing a public uproar that compelled the royal family to flee London. When civil war broke out a year later, the king's supporters at first enjoyed success but then suffered a series of defeats. The Puritan army, under Oliver Cromwell, was also winning a battle against Parliament's moderate members. Parliament charged Charles with treason, the first time in modern European history a monarch was brought to trial by his subjects. On January 27, 1649, the king was condemned, and on January 30, beheaded. During the final days of his imprisonment, he reportedly read plays by Shakespeare.

The property that had been home to the Globe was later absorbed into the grounds of a brewery. The only thing marking the site was a commemorative tablet on the brewery's walls, placed there by the Shakespeare Reading Society. For more than three hundred years, until the Globe was reconstructed just two hundred yards away, an entire "world" was lost.

EPILOGUE

Over the next three hundred years, such British celebrities as the actor David Garrick, poet Samuel Taylor Coleridge, and novelist William Makepeace Thackeray tried—unsuccessfully—to launch efforts to reconstruct the Globe at various times. While London remained without a Globe of its own, playhouses whose designs were inspired by the Globe sprang up all over the world. These playhouses may offer patrons upholstered seats and, in the case of the Tokyo Globe Theater, be constructed of salmon-pink concrete. But their polygonal forms all enclose tiered galleries facing a thrust stage, mimicking the Elizabethan Globe.

It was not until June 14, 1996, that a performance again took place at a Globe playhouse in London. Built in fulfillment of a dream of American actor Sam Wanamaker, the new Globe stands two hundred yards from the original site. As with the first Globe, oak timbers make up the frame. In addition, the foundation was laid in clay brick, rather than the concrete used for most buildings today. Lime plaster and sand cover the walls, and in a continued quest for authenticity, animal hair was mixed into the plaster. Plus, the roof was thatched by hand. The roof of the rebuilt Globe was in fact the first thatched roof in London since thatching was banned there following the Great Fire of 1666. To lessen the fire hazard, the thatching was treated with fire-retardant chemicals and a sprinkler system was installed.

Sam Wanamaker's dream of reconstructing the Globe came true when the playhouse was rebuilt just two hundred yards from its original site.

A bigger problem than complying with modern building codes to reconstruct the Globe was the absence of detailed plans of the original. Primary evidence is limited to drawings of the Globe's exterior seen on a few panoramic (or bird's-eye) views of London. Secondary evidence includes a sketch made from a foreign visitor's description of the interior of the Swan playhouse in 1596 and building contracts for two rival theaters, the Rose and the Fortune. More than one hundred scholars from around the world were therefore consulted on various aspects of the project.

Debate centered on whether the new Globe would operate as a museum to Elizabethan times or as a working professional theater. In other words, when remaining true to the original clashed with practicality, which would win out? At one point, for example, Sir Peter Hall, a founding director of Britain's Royal Shakespeare Company and a member of the board overseeing construction, insisted that the two large pillars supporting the canopy over the stage, as in the first Globe—which had been placed according to the sketch of the Swan—be repositioned to improve sight lines.

Throughout the reconstruction, doubts were raised about an Elizabethan-style public playhouse fitting in with the modern world. For one thing, the noise level in the area around the Globe is much greater than it was in the sixteenth and seventeenth centuries—especially since the playhouse now stands near one of the flight paths for London's Heathrow airport. Critics also questioned whether theater audiences accustomed to plush seats would put up with the discomfort of hard wood benches—let alone whether today's playgoers, their attention spans shortened by television, would endure the three-hours-plus length of traditional versions of Shakespeare's plays. "It may turn out to be a major tourist attraction," British playwright and screenwriter Tom Stoppard has said, "but that's got very little to do with contemporary theater."[64]

Although the rebuilt Globe has a thatched roof like the original, it is treated with fire-retardant chemicals and a sprinkler system to prevent destruction from another fire.

Its supporters admit that ticket sales alone will not meet the Globe's $1.5 million annual operating costs. For this reason, like the original Globe—whose profits included those from a neighboring inn—the new playhouse will not be in business by itself. Instead, the plan calls for the theater to be part of a complex known as the International Shakespeare Globe Center, scheduled to open in 1999. The center, when completed, is envisioned to include a multimedia resource library, museum, restaurant, and shops.

Despite the considerable costs—and controversy—surrounding the Globe's rebuilding, many are convinced of its value. Andrew Gurr, the chief scholarly adviser on reconstruction, explains,

The new Globe theater will be part of an International Shakespeare Globe Center, which will include a multimedia resource library, museum, restaurant, and shops.

"My analogy is really like having reconstructed the hardware in which we have to make Shakespeare's software work. The plays have been distorted by being put into modern theater, and I think this way of trying to approach the plays in their original tradition will be a . . . learning experience." [65] It will be a learning experience for those putting on the plays as well as for those in the audience. A remark by Globe actor Lennie James, following a performance of *Two Gentlemen of Verona*, that he has "never performed in any play where the audience became so vocally and physically involved" [66] was echoed by fellow actor Aicha Kossoko: "If the audience wasn't saying, 'Oh come on, give her a kiss,' they were booing and hissing." [67] Profitable or not, Shakespeare's Globe is no longer, in Hodges's words, a "missing monument of theatre history." [68] The Globe is once again a lively, colorful world.

NOTES

Please note that Elizabethan spellings in quoted material have been modernized when necessary for ease of reading.

Introduction

1. Peter Thomson, *Shakespeare's Theatre*. London: Routledge & Kegan Paul, 1983, p. 18.
2. Quoted in Michael Hattaway, *Elizabethan Popular Theatre: Plays in Performance*. Boston: Routledge & Kegan Paul, 1982, p. 33.

Chapter 1: Prologue

3. Quoted in Frances A. Yates, *Theatre of the World*. Chicago: University of Chicago Press, 1969, p. 113.
4. Quoted in Yates, *Theatre of the World*, p. 106.
5. Quoted in Richard Leacroft, *The Development of the English Playhouse*. Ithaca, NY: Cornell University Press, 1973, p. 26.
6. Simon Trussler, *The Cambridge Illustrated History of British Theatre*. Cambridge, England: Cambridge University Press, 1994, p. 71.
7. Trussler, *The Cambridge Illustrated History of British Theatre*, p. 69.
8. Quoted in Andrew Gurr, *The Shakespearean Stage: 1574–1642*. New York: Cambridge University Press, 1970, p. 87.
9. Quoted in Irwin Smith, *Shakespeare's Globe Playhouse: A Modern Reconstruction in Text and Scale Drawings*. New York: Charles Scribner's Sons, 1956, p. 5.
10. Quoted in Smith, *Shakespeare's Globe Playhouse*, p. 16.
11. Quoted in William Archer and W. J. Lawrence, "The Playhouse," *Shakespeare's England: An Account of the Life & Manners of His Age*, vol. 2. Oxford, England: Clarendon Press, 1966, p. 284.

Chapter 2: All the World's a Stage

12. Quoted in John Orrell, *The Quest for Shakespeare's Globe*. New York: Cambridge University Press, 1983, p. 111.
13. John Cranford Adams, *The Globe Playhouse: Its Design and Equipment*, 2nd ed. New York: Barnes & Noble, 1961, p. 24.
14. Smith, *Shakespeare's Globe Playhouse*, pp. 36–37.

15. Quoted in Smith, *Shakespeare's Globe Playhouse*, p. 34.

16. Smith, *Shakespeare's Globe Playhouse*, p. 36.

17. Quoted in Smith, *Shakespeare's Globe Playhouse*, p. 36.

18. Quoted in Smith, *Shakespeare's Globe Playhouse*, p. 69.

19. Quoted in C. Walter Hodges, *The Globe Restored: A Study of the Elizabethan Theatre.* New York: Coward-McCann, 1954, p. 41.

20. Quoted in Adams, *The Globe Playhouse*, p. 104.

21. Quoted in Richard Covington, "The Rebirth of Shakespeare's Globe," *Smithsonian*, November 1997, p. 70.

22. Quoted in Barry Day, *This Wooden "O": Shakespeare's Globe Reborn.* New York: Limelight Editions, 1998, p. 255.

Chapter 3: The Play's the Thing

23. Quoted in Adams, *The Globe Playhouse*, p. 379.

24. Quoted in Adams, *The Globe Playhouse*, p. 106.

25. Quoted in Gerald Eades Bentley, *The Jacobean and Caroline Stage,* vol. 6, *Theatres.* Oxford, England: Clarendon Press, 1968, p. 184.

26. Quoted in Andrew Gurr, *Playgoing in Shakespeare's London.* New York: Cambridge University Press, 1987, p. 214.

27. Quoted in Gurr, *Playgoing in Shakespeare's London*, p. 228.

28. Covington, "The Rebirth of Shakespeare's Globe," p. 66.

29. Quoted in Thomson, *Shakespeare's Theatre*, p. 11.

30. Quoted in Bernard Beckerman, *Shakespeare at the Globe, 1599–1609.* New York: Macmillan, 1962, p. 67.

31. Quoted in Beckerman, *Shakespeare at the Globe, 1599–1609*, p. 67.

32. Quoted in A. M. Nagler, *Shakespeare's Stage.* New Haven, CT: Yale University Press, 1958, p. 33.

33. Quoted in Hodges, *The Globe Restored*, p. 51.

34. Quoted in Hattaway, *Elizabethan Popular Theatre*, p. 38.

35. Quoted in Harold Burris-Meyer and Edward C. Cole, *Theatres and Auditoriums,* 2nd ed. New York: Reinhold, 1964, p. 171.

36. Quoted in Smith, *Shakespeare's Globe Playhouse*, p. 147.

37. Quoted in Gerald Eades Bentley, "The Theatres and the Actors," part 3 of *The Revels History of Drama in English,* vol. 4, *1613–1660.* New York: Methuen, 1981, p. 166.

Chapter 4: Debits and Credits

38. Thomson, *Shakespeare's Theatre*, pp. 63–64.

39. Quoted in Thomson, *Shakespeare's Theatre*, p. 66.

40. Quoted in Thomson, *Shakespeare's Theatre*, p. 70.

41. Quoted in Thomson, *Shakespeare's Theatre*, p. 70.

42. Quoted in Gurr, *The Shakespearean Stage*, p. 93.

43. Quoted in Thomson, *Shakespeare's Theatre*, p. 69.

44. Quoted in Gurr, *Playgoing in Shakespeare's London*, p. 236.

45. Quoted in Thomson, *Shakespeare's Theatre*, p. 8.

46. Quoted in Gerald Eades Bentley, *The Jacobean and Caroline Stage*, vol. 1, *Dramatic Companies and Players*. Oxford, England: Clarendon Press, 1941, pp. 55–56.

47. Quoted in Bentley, *The Jacobean and Caroline Stage*, vol. 1, p. 27.

48. Quoted in Bentley, *The Jacobean and Caroline Stage*, vol. 1, p. 21.

49. Quoted in Archer and Lawrence, "The Playhouse," p. 284.

50. Quoted in Bentley, "The Theatres and the Actors," pp. 77–78.

51. Quoted in Bentley, "The Theatres and the Actors," p. 78.

52. Quoted in Orrell, *The Quest for Shakespeare's Globe*, p. 121.

Chapter 5: The Comeback

53. Quoted in Bentley, *The Jacobean and Caroline Stage*, vol. 6, p. 182.

54. Quoted in Orrell, *The Quest for Shakespeare's Globe*, p. 121.

55. Quoted in Bentley, *The Jacobean and Caroline Stage*, vol. 6, p. 182.

56. Quoted in Bentley, *The Jacobean and Caroline Stage*, vol. 6, p. 182.

57. Quoted in Gurr, *Playgoing in Shakespeare's London*, p. 189.

58. Quoted in Bentley, *The Jacobean and Caroline Stage*, vol. 1, p. 12.

59. Quoted in Bentley, *The Jacobean and Caroline Stage*, vol. 1, p. 61.

60. Quoted in Adams, *The Globe Playhouse*, p. 379.

61. Quoted in Bentley, *The Jacobean and Caroline Stage*, vol. 1, p. 67.

62. Quoted in Bentley, *The Jacobean and Caroline Stage*, vol. 1, pp. 67–68.

63. Quoted in Bentley, *The Jacobean and Caroline Stage*, vol. 1, pp. 68–69.

Epilogue

64. Quoted in William Triplett, "The Globe, As Who Likes It? Authenticity vs. Practicality at the Site of the Reconstruction of Shakespeare's Globe Theater," *Washington Post*, December 17, 1995, p. G2.

65. Quoted in Triplett, "The Globe, As Who Likes It?" p. G2.

66. Quoted in Covington, "The Rebirth of Shakespeare's Globe," p. 66.

67. Quoted in Covington, "The Rebirth of Shakespeare's Globe," p. 74.

68. C. Walter Hodges, *Shakespeare's Second Globe: The Missing Monument*, London: Oxford University Press, 1973, p. 16.

For Further Reading

John Russell Brown, *Shakespeare and His Theater.* New York: Lothrop, Lee & Shepard Books, 1982. Clearly presented, engaging description of the construction and operation of the Globe by a well-known Shakespearean scholar. Many illustrations.

C. Walter Hodges, *Shakespeare's Theatre.* New York: Coward-McCann, 1964. Lively account of theatergoing in Shakespeare's time. Color drawings by the author.

Horizon Magazine, *Shakespeare's England.* New York: American Heritage, 1964. An overview of the Elizabethan period that offers lots of illustrations and vivid detail. Some coverage of the Globe.

Jacqueline Morley, *Shakespeare's Theater.* New York: Peter Bedrick Books, 1994. An introduction to the Globe, organized by topic. Fully illustrated, with most of the text in caption form. Includes glossary.

Diane Yancey, *Life in the Elizabethan Theater.* San Diego: Lucent Books, 1997. Comprehensive look at English theater in the fifteenth century, with one chapter devoted to playhouses, including the Globe. Plenty of illustrations.

Works Consulted

Books

John Cranford Adams, *The Globe Playhouse: Its Design and Equipment.* 2nd ed. New York: Barnes & Noble, 1961. Although Adams's reconstruction has been disputed by later scholars, he provides much primary-source material, which adds color and detail to the story of the building of the Globe. Often technical.

William Archer and W. J. Lawrence, "The Playhouse," *Shakespeare's England: An Account of the Life & Manners of His Age.* Vol. 2. Oxford, England: Clarendon Press, 1966. Presents a lot of information concisely, though the section on staging techniques is mostly outdated. For its length, a good resource for firsthand accounts.

Bernard Beckerman, *Shakespeare at the Globe, 1599–1609.* New York: Macmillan, 1962. A thorough investigation of how plays were staged at the Globe, shedding light on the theater's design.

Gerald Eades Bentley, *The Jacobean and Caroline Stage.* Vol. 1, *Dramatic Companies and Players.* Oxford, England: Clarendon Press, 1941. Chronicles in detail the history of the King's Men, starting from 1616 to the troupe's end. Especially valuable in researching finances regarding the Globe.

———, *The Jacobean and Caroline Stage.* Vol. 6, *Theatres.* Oxford, England: Clarendon Press, 1968. A brief but detailed survey of the second Globe, with occasional reference to the first.

———, "The Theatres and the Actors," part 3 of *The Revels History of Drama in English.* Vol. 4, *1613–1660.* New York: Methuen, 1981. Provides a comprehensive history of the King's Men during the period of the second Globe.

Martin S. Briggs, *The Architect in History.* New York: Da Capo Press, 1974. A thorough discussion of how the profession of architect evolved in Europe. A chapter is devoted to the Renaissance in England.

Harold Burris-Meyer and Edward C. Cole, *Theatres and Auditoriums,* 2nd ed. New York: Reinhold, 1964. A textbook on theater design, with emphasis on modern construction. Some description of the workings of a trap and flying mechanism; technical.

Elizabeth Burton, *The Pageant of Elizabethan England.* New York: Charles Scribner's Sons, 1958. An entertaining survey of the daily lives of Elizabethans. Offers fascinating details on architecture, manners, and pastimes, with some discussion of playgoing.

Marchette Chute, *Shakespeare of London.* New York: E. P. Dutton, 1949. With the skill of a novelist, the author describes the life of Shakespeare as a working man of the theater in Elizabethan London. Other members of the Globe's company of players are portrayed, too.

Barry Day, *This Wooden "O": Shakespeare's Globe Reborn.* New York: Limelight Editions, 1998. The story of the rebuilding of the Globe told with documentary-like detail by an insider: the director of the International Shakespeare Globe Centre. Historical, architectural, and political considerations are presented in a very readable way.

Andrew Gurr, *The Shakespearean Stage: 1574–1642.* New York: Cambridge University Press, 1970. An overview of the playhouses of the period, including the Globe. Gurr was a primary authority in the project to reconstruct the Globe in London.

———, *Playgoing in Shakespeare's London.* New York: Cambridge University Press, 1987. A thorough investigation of the experience of attending plays in Elizabethan times, with lots of lively detail. An appendix includes pages of contemporary references to playgoing, many of them humorous.

Michael Hattaway, *Elizabethan Popular Theatre: Plays in Performance.* Boston: Routledge & Kegan Paul, 1982. A survey of the Elizabethan playhouse with much reference to the Globe. Well balanced regarding controversies over playhouse design and staging of plays.

C. Walter Hodges, *The Globe Restored: A Study of the Elizabethan Theatre.* New York: Coward-McCann, 1954. An imagined reconstruction of the Globe by a stage designer with practical experience in theater. Numerous illustrations, including many by Hodges himself. A number of appendixes offer details about Elizabethan public playhouses.

————, *Shakespeare's Second Globe: The Missing Monument.* London: Oxford University Press, 1973. A convincing reconstruction of the second Globe. Technical at times, but with many illustrations.

Richard Hosley, "The Playhouses," part 3 of *The* Revels *History of Drama in English.* Vol. 3, *1576–1613.* London: Methuen, 1975. Building suspense, the author tests his theories regarding the design of the first Globe with reference to plays known to have been performed there. Several drawings detail the theater's structural frame.

George C. Izenour, *Theater Design.* New York: McGraw-Hill, 1972. Thorough analysis of theater design, including discussion of sight and hearing lines. Includes a summary of Vetruvius's theory of theater construction as well as a brief analysis of the Globe. Very technical.

Richard Leacroft, *The Development of the English Playhouse.* Ithaca, NY: Cornell University Press, 1973. A straightforward illustrated history of playhouse design in Britain. Includes a reconstruction of the second Globe, in theory.

A. M. Nagler, *Shakespeare's Stage.* New Haven, CT: Yale University Press, 1958. In fewer than a hundred pages, reviews the available evidence on the Globe's interior and how plays were staged there. Features a description of a performance of Shakespeare's *Romeo and Juliet* at the Globe, based on the author's conclusions.

John Orrell, *The Quest for Shakespeare's Globe.* New York: Cambridge University Press, 1983. Details the construction of the Globe, arguing persuasively for a design based on Tudor tools and traditions. Provides illustrations, but technical.

Irwin Smith, *Shakespeare's Globe Playhouse: A Modern Reconstruction in Text and Scale Drawings.* New York: Charles Scribner's Sons, 1956. Smith participated in building the scale model, based on John Cranford Adams's reconstruction of the Globe, housed at the Shakespeare Folger Library in Washington, D.C. So although he offers much practical detail about building techniques and design, his description of staging is outdated. Very useful in understanding Tudor carpentry.

Peter Thomson, *Shakespeare's Theatre*. London: Routledge & Kegan Paul, 1983. Comprehensive account of the first Globe, written in a lively style. Provides hypothetical stagings of Shakepeare's plays *Macbeth* and *As You Like It*.

Simon Trussler, *The Cambridge Illustrated History of British Theatre*. Cambridge, England: Cambridge University Press, 1994. A very readable history of theater in Britain. Provides much background material as well as up-to-date research.

Charles William Wallace, *The First London Theatre: Materials for a History*. Reprint. New York: Benjamin Blom, 1969. A collection of fascinating primary-source documents chronicling the legal and business conflicts surrounding James Burbage's Theatre. An introduction presents an often amusing history of these tensions, leading to the building of the Globe.

Frances A. Yates, *Theatre of the World*. Chicago: University of Chicago Press, 1969. Argues passionately for the basis of the Globe's design in classicism. Also suggests a metaphysical significance to the design that is highly speculative if intriguing.

Periodicals

Richard Covington, "The Rebirth of Shakespeare's Globe," *Smithsonian*, November 1997.

Dan Cruikshank, "Shakespeare on the Thames," *Progressive Architecture*, May 1995.

William Triplett, "The Globe, As Who Likes It? Authenticity vs. Practicality at the Site of the Reconstruction of Shakespeare's Globe Theater," *Washington Post*, December 17, 1995.

INDEX

PICTURE CREDITS

ABOUT THE AUTHOR

A daughter of performers, Amy Allison has long felt at home in theaters. A great believer in the showmanship of Shakespeare, her love of his plays comes above all from experiencing them onstage, in performance. Allison grew up in and around Washington, D.C., where she and her classmates went on numerous field trips to buildings whose histories are interwoven with the history of the United States. She now lives in the Los Angeles area with her husband, Dave Edison, who is employed in the entertainment industry. Allison's other nonfiction titles include *Gargoyles on Guard,* and her poetry has appeared in *Jack & Jill* and *Cricket* magazines.